"Guisinger's honesty had me from the get-go. Read it, fall in love as I did, learn something you may not yet know. Did I mention Penny Guisinger is also very funny? She is also very funny."

—**Abigail Thomas**, author of *Still Life at Eighty:*
*The Next Interesting Thing*

"What I love most about this smart, edgy memoir is how it celebrates love, in all its permutations, how in it, who we love and how are more important than what we are called, than what we call ourselves. It imagines a world that accepts that to be human is to shift, where a foreshortened marriage is not a failure but a limited success, where it is possible to find safety, self, a path through our altering personal geometries to a place where we can love intelligently, with candor and without masks."

—**Pam Houston**, author of *Deep Creek: Finding*
*Hope in the High Country*

"Each sentence in this book is a delightful jewel, and the sum of these sentences asks, 'What is time? Am I the selves I was, who I pretended to be, and the selves that have grown into the present?' Guisinger tracks love and days as they wink and flitter within and beyond timelines and roles, creating a breathtaking quantum nonfiction portrait."

—**Sonya Huber**, author of *Pain Woman Takes Your Keys,*
*and Other Essays from a Nervous System*

"I read *Shift* with my heart in my throat. It's both the most romantic book I've encountered in ages and a clear-eyed dissection of romance's consequences when falling in love means reinventing not just a life but a self. This urgent, wry, deeply reflective book will be with me for a long time."

—**Kristi Coulter**, author of *Nothing Good Can Come from This*

"*Shift* is the story of hard-won love, told with an honesty that includes heartbroken children, sexual euphoria, and the crooked road toward remaking a family."

—**Monica Wood**, author of *When We Were the Kennedys: A Memoir from Mexico, Maine*

"In *Shift* Penny Guisinger takes us on a lyrical journey to self. And it's a beautiful story: a young teen groping for identity—a queer identity—grows into a self-possessed, independent woman negotiating family and friendship, career and romance, mind-work and hard physical work. By turns harrowing, hilarious, erotic, wise, and calm, honest and cagey, poetic and profound, *Shift* is a joy to read, and Penny Guisinger a delightful storyteller and thinker. Don't start the book late at night; you'll get less sleep than Penny during a first lesbian encounter. Yes, those are birds singing, and we've spent the night in bliss."

—**Bill Roorbach**, author of *Summers with Juliet, Lucky Turtle*, and *Beep*

"Using the poetics of mathematics as her touchstone, Penny Guisinger has woven a captivating tale of love and desire, harmony and dissonance, fracture and repair. This book is a window into a critical point in queer history, when gay marriage was legal in some states but not yet all, a story told by a woman who did not discover she was gay until several years after she was a mother married to a man. Read this book. It's like nothing you've ever read before."

—**Jennifer Lunden**, author of *American Breakdown*

"As with a walk along the lengths and curves of a Mobius strip, Penny Guisinger didn't complete the path of this story the same person she was at the start. Nor will you."

—**Suzanne Strempk Shea**, author of *Sundays in America: A Yearlong Road Trip in Search of Christian Faith*

# Shift

American Lives    *Series editor:* Tobias Wolff

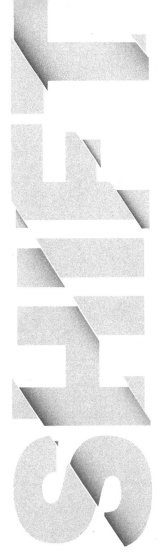

A memoir of identity
and other illusions

PENNY GUISINGER

University of Nebraska Press    *Lincoln*

Earlier versions of "Provincetown I" and
"Provincetown II" appeared as "Provincetown"
in *Solstice Literary Magazine*, August 7, 2013. An
earlier version of "Coming Out" appeared in
*Fourth Genre* 16, no. 2 (2014). An earlier version
of "Is This Parenting?" appeared as "I Have This
Part Right" in *River Teeth* 15, no. 2 (2014).

The University of Nebraska Press is part of a
land-grant institution with campuses and programs
on the past, present, and future homelands of
the Pawnee, Ponca, Otoe-Missouria, Omaha,
Dakota, Lakota, Kaw, Cheyenne, and Arapaho
Peoples, as well as those of the relocated
Ho-Chunk, Sac and Fox, and Iowa Peoples.

Library of Congress
Cataloging-in-Publication Data
Names: Guisinger, Penny, author.
Title: Shift: a memoir of identity and
other illusions / Penny Guisinger.
Description: Lincoln: University of Nebraska
Press, [2024] | Series: American lives
Identifiers: LCCN 2023037631
ISBN 9781496238900 (paperback)
ISBN 9781496239860 (epub)
ISBN 9781496239877 (pdf)
Subjects: LCSH: Sex. | Sexual minorities—
Biography. | Gender identity. | Marriage.
Classification: LCC HQ21 .G835 2024 |
DDC 306.76—dc23/eng/20230902
LC record available at
https://lccn.loc.gov/2023037631

Designed and set in Janson Text by L. Welch.

To my dad,
who made me an artist.

To my mom,
who made me a fighter.

To Abby and Owen,
who made me a
bigger, better person.


To Karabird,
who sings to me.

# AUTHOR'S NOTE

Every event in this story is real, and this is my version of those events. I have done my best to capture the story sincerely and honestly. Others may remember things differently. If so, maybe they will write their own book. I hope they do.

Everyone in this story is a real person. In some cases, names have been changed.

Shift

# Shift and Back Up

Kara and I like implementers and persuaders made of steel, like hammers and pry bars, saws and wrenches. We like equipment and dirt. We like weekend projects. I like to put on leather work gloves, lower the tongue of our utility trailer onto my car's ball hitch, drop the safety chains into the rust-crusted holes, and turn the stubborn knob, tightening the rig into a locked position, ready to haul firewood, the rototiller, or loam. I like to do these things wearing a ball cap and a work shirt with ripped-out elbows.

Kara found the utility trailer on Craig's List. It was an incredible deal. Black steel with rugged tires and a two-bar rail around three sides, worth the two-hour trip through the woods to Bangor, Maine, to meet the guy in a strip mall parking lot, where we handed him cash and switched the trailer from his car to mine. Having a hitch installed on my Honda cost as much as the trailer itself, but we wanted it. We didn't predict that the trailer would be the thing that revealed our deficiencies. Hadn't we already logged enough self-improvement hours that year? We should have been perfect.

All that summer, the trailer bumped along behind us, hauling seaweed and composted manure from the organic dairy farm across the bay. We had mowed and tilled a large rectangle of field outside our house, and by amending it with nutrients and microorganisms, we negotiated with that clay earth until it turned into soil. We loaded the trailer with pitchfork loads of dripping, rotting sugar kelp, bladderwort, sea lettuce, and dulse harvested from below the high-water mark on the boat ramp, then drove home and spread it across the garden. We hoisted pointy shovels to slop globs of cow manure from the trailer's deck, tried not to inhale the smell as we pushed it into the place where tomatoes would grow. We wore caps and gloves and down vests and jeans and work boots. Flannel and serious expressions.

The Honda CRV, with its five-speed, standard transmission, was chosen to pull the trailer, as it was the larger and more powerful of our two vehicles. This was fine, except that I did not know how to back the trailer down the boat ramp, across the yard into the garden, or anywhere else. Backing up a trailer is a process of counterintuitive thinking and spatial relations that I wasn't born with. Now I know to grab the steering wheel with one hand at the six o'clock position and to move that hand whichever direction I want the back of the trailer to go, but that skill was yet to come. Kara, on the other hand, could back up a trailer but had never learned the ballet of integrating her two feet, the car's three pedals, the steering wheel, and the stick.

But we were innovators. We designed a system. To back up, we would park the car, unhitch the trailer, and maneuver it into position by hand. Then I would back the car up to the stationary trailer, and we would lift and reattach. No problem.

That worked for the summer, but our unskillfulness would not be bypassed forever. One fall day, we had the trailer loaded with seaweed, and we struggled to move it into the garden. I had driven close to the edge of the tilled ground, near where the kale would grow in the spring. Kara held the trailer tongue from one side, and I had a glove-covered hold from the other, and we tried to drag it across a bumpy section of ground between my car and the garden. Its large, black tires sank into a low spot, and we threw all the strength in our bodies into hauling it up over the lip. It resisted and tugged back, wrestling itself out of our hands. The steel tongue of the fully loaded trailer dropped directly onto the top of my foot.

I sank to the ground, unable to speak. Kara jumped to get my foot free. I lay on the ground, eyes closed, while Kara slid the trailer off my thin, rubber boot, then the boot off my foot. She said, "Don't move."

We stayed there for a minute, me on my back, her holding my throbbing foot on her bent knee. Around us, birds that hadn't left with the summer sang their autumn songs and clouds slid across an expanse of sky. I finally managed to say, "That landed on my foot."

She stroked my calf. "I know."

The ground was soft, and the trailer had pushed my foot into the mud rather than breaking the bones, but it was badly bruised. We had traveled rougher terrain, hauling heavier loads, but we weren't done.

I had to learn to back up and shift at the same time.

# PART 1

# Imperfect Rings

Sitting cross-legged on a bed in a Super 8 motel, I am following instructions on the internet in a weird, desperate exercise to get my hands around my story in a physical way: to create something I can hang above my desk as a reminder that beginnings are often indistinguishable from middles, and sometimes there's no ending. I cut two thin strips of paper, then tape their ends together to make two separate rings, then start cutting the third. Borromean rings are mathematical impossibilities: three perfect rings linked in such a way that if you cut one, all three fall away from each other. They can be drawn but cannot be created in real life without warping at least one of the circles. To interlock, one of them must cock a hip or shift its weight to the other foot.

I tried for years to impose order on this story. I conceptualized it as a tryptic: before, during, and after. Humans like sets of three. We like musketeers, blind mice, little pigs, wise men, rings in a circus, sheets to the wind, pieces in a suit, little kittens, legged races, and bears. Ready, set, go. Rock, paper, scissors. Bacon, lettuce, tomato. Life, liberty, happiness. Stop, drop, roll. Location, location, location. Wine, women, song. Father, son, holy spirit. Students of writing, painting, and public speaking are taught the rule of three, which says that three is intrinsically more satisfying than four or two. Nobody knows why this is true.

The bedspread in the Super 8 is patterned with blue circles of assorted sizes overlapping and intersecting over a brown background. I cut a third strip of paper. Using an online illustration as a guide, I slide it over one ring, under another, back over the first one, then under the last one, then I tape its ends together, and I find that it's true. The three paper rings are a little lumpy and weird looking, but they are joined in a three-dimensional, three-part telling of something that cannot be depicted with one straight line. The strips of paper, no matter how they have been turned and looped into this new form, are still strips of paper.

A Mobius strip might be a better expression of this story than a set of three rings if not for its status as a two-dimensional phenomenon. It has no boundaries, no beginning, no end, and cannot be oriented. If you were to become two-dimensional and walk the length of a Mobius strip, you would end up where you started, but the trip would involve some trickery and for a time you would be upside down. For a time, you would be a mirror image of yourself existing on the same surface as the original you. When you reached the end—also known as the beginning—you would find yourself exactly as you started but perhaps different for the flopping about you experienced along the way. A German-born mathematician named Burkard Polster, who runs a YouTube channel called *Mathologer*, describes the trip around the Mobius strip like this: "You won't feel it. You will feel perfectly fine all the way throughout the trip, but you come back strange." Polster tries to explain that it's possible that you will return from a trip around the half-turn as a mirror image of yourself. A trip with no edges, with only one surface, one direction, can flip us around but leave us otherwise intact.

I adjust my position on the bedspread and take one breath to realize that the number 8 in the Super 8 logo is also composed of rings. It's possible I'm thinking too much. My misshapen, crinkly set of Borromean rings dangles from my hand in the dim motel room light.

# We Were Just Rehearsing

I was having phone sex with a girl who was not named Grace (but that is what we will call her for now) throughout high school, and sometimes reaching under her shirt in person, but I never thought of myself as anything other than straight. As we breathed heavily into the phone, describing all the things we imagined ourselves doing to one another, we were pretending to be other people, so it didn't count. We were going to be famous actors. We were rehearsing.

"I want you," I said to Grace, lying on my bed in my room with the phone against my head.

"What do you want to do to me?" I knew she had the phone dragged into her room. The cord was twisted and tangled under the closed door.

"I think you know. I'm taking your shirt off." I breathed these words into the receiver. "And now I'm inside you. Right *now*." Alone in my room, my hips moved accordingly.

Grace moaned softly. "I love you."

She had a delicate, bird-like face, with a sharp nose and chin, and she wore huge, round glasses. I was sure I was not attracted to her, but I took every opportunity to explore her body, mostly through her clothes, when nobody else was home. Usually, we went out together, to Greenwich Village. We spent afternoons wandering the stretch of Broadway between the Strand and Tower Records. We played roles, adopted other personas. If we could arrange it, if her mother wasn't home, we went back to their apartment and got into bed. In these games, I sometimes played the female characters, but I only ever wanted to play the men. I wanted to pretend to want women.

Many years later, at the age of fifty-one, I read the memoir *Blow Your House Down* by Gina Frangello. Until then, I had assumed that the elaborate games of make-believe Grace and I played were indicative of something deeply wrong with both of us, and since I felt like the instigator, there was something extra deeply wrong with me. Frangello writes about playing "Karen and Genevieve" with her childhood friend Alicia. She also writes about assigning alternate identities and names to every one of her classmates and making up elaborate stories about these imaginary versions of real people. Further, she writes about returning to this refuge in adulthood, pretending to be Mary, the protagonist of a novel she was writing. "But at the age of forty-two, on a bucket-list dream trip in Kenya with your family, you are still pretending to be Mary, dividing your attention between what is real and what is not, that old equator you cannot seem to stop straddling. . . . You are old enough to know that at this point you are exercising choice—that you are voluntarily participating when you could just stop. But you do not stop." I was struck numb by the realization that Grace and I were not the only ones, and that maybe whatever was deeply wrong with me was as deeply wrong with others. Or maybe it wasn't deeply wrong at all.

Like Gina and Alicia, Grace and I had a cast of characters we rotated through, each with complex back stories and relationships with each other. Some were based on characters from television shows or movies. Others were celebrities we wished we could be friends with. Others still were characters from the pages of terrible fiction writing I did in high school and college. When Grace and I were in bed together, it wasn't really us: it was Benji and Janet (two rock stars) or Thompson and Michelle (an FBI agent and his wife) or Billy Joel and Christie Brinkley. I suppose it made the not-quite-sex feel not-quite-real, given our plans to evolve into Grace and Penny (an actress and a novelist) of the future. We carried the game everywhere we went, even when we weren't together. We had phone calls in which our characters spoke to each other, and when I went to college upstate our characters exchanged long letters sent through the mail. I have a memory of my old word processor chugging out fifteen or twenty single-spaced pages of "Dear Janet/Dear Michelle/Dear Christie" letters. I mailed them to Brooklyn in fat envelopes and waited eagerly for the responses. I was certain, at the time, that no other almost-adults were engaging in such nonsense, but now I'm not so sure.

In my memory, the apartment Grace lived in with her mother was always dark and filled with belongings stored in plastic bags stacked to the ceiling. We used to lie together on her mother's bed, pretending to be the straight, married adults populating our fantasy world. One afternoon, her sharp hip bone was against my belly as she pressed against me from underneath, and I put my hand on her stomach. Our clothes never came off. We never reached into each other. I remember the feeling of her fingers around my wrist, though, and her breath against my neck. She was flat-chested, and I was not, and my breasts pressed against her ribcage. Outside, the Brooklyn neighborhood made its noises. Cars eased past, sometimes honking at people on the sidewalk. Mothers and grandmothers pulled their two-wheeled grocery carts up and down the sidewalk. Teenagers coolly strode by, running their hands along the rungs of the painted, wrought-iron fence outside the apartment. Her glasses sat on the nightstand. We breathed and talked our way through acts we could not perform, as if we were still on the phone.

"I love being inside you."

"You fill me up."

"Don't stop," she said, with a sharp intake of breath. "Don't ever stop."

These things we said in this imaginary world were the way we imagined love to be. They were lines passed back and forth like smooth subway tokens, the entrance to someplace we had never been. And yet, despite all these words and all the illicit touching and panting, real-me was not in love with real-Grace. I was too busy nurturing the crushes I had on boys in my high school. I was straight.

Back then, New York City eighth graders could opt out of attending the zoned high school in their own neighborhood by taking a placement test to see if they might qualify for one of the specialized high schools located across the boroughs. Some schools offered focused areas of study like math, medicine, or acting, and some didn't but were still seen as better options than the zoned schools. While that admissions system is now right-fully imperiled by its own carefully coded racism, at the time all I cared about was going someplace where I might have a social life and a good chance at college.

Grace and I both tested out of our zoned school, and she went to John Dewey while I went to Midwood, and because these schools were separated by multiple neighborhoods, I was able to carefully control how often and under what circumstances we saw each other. I did not invite her to Midwood parties. I believed, therefore, that I was the only one in control, keeping this friendship stored in a closet, protecting my straightness by hiding this other thing, but now I realize I never saw the inside of a John Dewey party either. Midwood was somewhere in the middle of the upper tier of prestigious high schools. It was for kids who were smart but not smart enough to get into Stuyvesant. Though Dewey was not the high school Grace was zoned for, it was still somewhere below Midwood on this phony intellectual hierarchy. Adolescence is two-dimensional in some ways—more timeline than geometry. At a time in our lives when we desperately need human connection and compassion, we are least equipped to provide it to each other. I was Grace's friend, but I was not especially nice to her. I did not want her hanging around with my mid-upper-tier-high-school-but-not-good-enough-for-Stuyvesant friends. My status was tenuous enough without this liability.

Grace was, I now know, a kinder person than I was, with an innocence that I envy today. Proud to be a Brooklyn girl, she never went on to live anywhere else. At the time, what I knew was that she had this full-body laugh that burst from her when the jokes weren't even that funny. Taller than me and impossibly skinny, she was all bones and sharp angles. The lenses of her glasses were thick, and in the large, round frames that were popular at the time, they magnified her eyes, giving her an amazed, surprised expression.

She kept a pile of movie magazines next to her bed, with svelte actresses in tight dresses in or on the arms of barely shaved actors. We sat on her bed one afternoon, paging through them. Her mom was in the living room watching television, so we kept our hands off each other. Grace believed that someday I would be famous. She believed that all the research and rehearsing we were doing would lead me to write a commercially powerful screenplay or novel or both. As we flipped the glossy magazine pages, our fingers sliding across the pictures, she said, "Maybe someday Harrison Ford will be in your movie."

In my memory, her bedroom was small and windowless, but perceptions like that are made suspect by how corruptible our memories are. Self-servitude and the need to make every remembered image match the way a thing felt can shove the wrong images into what become static, fragmented snapshots. I believe her room was meant to be a large, walk-in closet, located as it was, directly off her mom's bedroom. It was the sort of room that new parents might make into a nursery for a baby. It wasn't big enough for a teenager, but New York City apartment living is like living aboard a sailboat: everything is tiny and cramped, and people get creative about using their spaces. But maybe her room was not a closet at all. Maybe that's a memory about being in a different kind of closet entirely.

Grace's room was an avalanche of stuff. Clothes, stuffed animals, magazines, and records stacked up the walls, forming impossible-looking mountain ranges. She was fond of big plastic key chains, rabbits' feet, and pin-on buttons with slogans like, "I love soaps."

I sat on her bed with my back against the wall. "That would be cool," I said, less convinced that anything I wrote would ever get the attention of anyone beyond the two of us. I wrote short stories then and had a novel in progress. It was exactly the sort of novel one expects from a geeky teenage outcast: a manuscript full of adventure, romance, and intrigue. The short stories were about sensitive men, able to express their feelings, men possessing all the qualities that teenage boys lack, all the qualities that I later discovered in women. All the qualities that were sitting next to me that I was too embarrassed to see.

Like Gina Frangello and her friend Alicia, Grace and I eventually stopped our game, though all these years later I'm not sure I can pinpoint when or why. Like Frangello, I occasionally drifted back into the game into middle age. I leaned into these fictions when real life was too complicated to understand or too painful to stay in. I lay in bed imagining myself trapped in a wrecked car, or I shopped for groceries pretending I had just been released from jail or rehab. "Inside the confines of another fictional woman's skin, you cannot be hurt; you cannot be disappointed; you cannot wonder why you are putting up with behavior you orchestrated your entire life in an attempt to flee," writes Frangello. "Yes, you remember this: the oblivion, more soothing than rum and gingers, better than any drug you've ever tried. The water is always warm in here. Come in." Alicia eventually tells Frangello that "when you played the male characters, she found you attractive and felt like she had a crush on you. Maybe it was the reason you stopped. You had reached an age where the Imaginary could no longer exist without the erotic."

# Bonking into Each Other in the Dark

As students in history class, we learn to consider that major events can be placed on a linear timeline. This thing happens. Then that. Then the next thing. Anything that happened in 1999 is ten clicks back from events of 2019. I strive to believe that the relationship with Grace happened so long ago it's as if it happened to somebody else. I was fifteen when we met, and thirty-eight when I shifted into this fully gay life, and I prefer to consider that block of twenty-three years as a solid, discreet unit, safely behind me, but it's generally accepted in physics that time is a construction that exists in a weird, multidimensional box. The truth might be that all the events that have ever happened circle around each other in a four-dimensional space, bonking into each other in the dark. Physicists, who think about such things, demand that I consider the feeling of that sharp hip bone pressing into my body as something that has not disappeared into the nothingness of the past. Time is a topography, not a list. Grace, along with the boys and men who came after her, may be standing across the room from me, drifting in our time-box; we try awkwardly to avoid each other because what is there to say now?

# Before There Was a Woman

It was 1986. A decades-old bing cherry tree shaded the small square that we called the backyard. Henry picked up a cherry pit, let it drop into his palm, and then did it again until he had a small collection of the sticky orbs, black with dried juice. Then he tossed them, one at a time, through the chain-link fence that separated my yard from the above-ground portion of the New York City subway tracks. He talked about Lucy, and I listened. Our conversation was interrupted by the sound of the D train rocketing past, filling the air with a crashing, clacketing violence of sound, then dropping us back into the relative peace of the neighborhood. We sat on the concrete stoop on the back of my parents' house, tossing cherry pits, discussing the sadness in Henry's life that was his girlfriend, and my good friend, Lucy.

We were maybe sixteen, and the situation seemed grave. Henry was the first of a string of boys that I was friends with but wanted to be more. Through high school and college and the years in between college and grad school there was a series of boys like Henry in my life: wounded, brooding, and out of reach.

"I love her," Henry said, squinting up at the flat steel wall of the subway station, twenty yards beyond the fence. In the space beneath that wall, the shoes of people waiting for the next local shifted and scuffed. I pictured them leaning out over the track, just a little farther off the edge of the platform than they should, straining to see the train coming.

"Of course," I said, nudging a cherry seed forward with the toe of my sneaker. I wore white Tretorns with a blue accent. They matched Billy Joel's sneakers, and that was important.

Lucy was a blonde cheerleader, and I mean that in the worst possible way. She was the teenage girl whose saggy cotton sweaters were always the same color as the baggy cotton socks we all wore that year to approximate leg warmers. She was thin but not athletic, smart but not brilliant, and unlike most of my friends, she had a serious boyfriend.

My friends and I were not the cool kids, and none of us (except Lucy) had boyfriends. I had no claim to any of the popular groups in school, and judging by photos from that time, my clothes were curated to ensure that I would never be mistaken for someone seeking to fit in. One outfit was a flowery skirt worn over a pair of long underwear and a surgical scrub shirt over a long-sleeved Lake Placid T-shirt. I did okay within my small sphere of friends, but there was no boyfriend forthcoming.

"Do you know what she calls me now? Like it's my new nickname?" Henry had dark blond hair, the color of hay, beagle-brown eyes, and full lips. He looked at his palm load of cherry pits, like maybe they held some information that would help.

I knew about the new nickname. Lucy had told me about it when we changed for gym class. I had also heard about it from our friend Anna, who was there when it happened. But I didn't want Henry to know that I knew, so I said, "No. What do you mean?" while I reached down to flick off a cherry seed that had fallen from Henry's hand onto my stark white sneaker. It left a red smudge on the toe.

"She's calling me 'Unwanted Baby' now."

Everyone knew Henry was adopted, but it came up at a party, and if you believed Anna, Lucy spent that whole night taunting him about it because it suited Anna to put Lucy in the worst light; if you believed Henry, this had softened into some kinder form of teasing because it suited him to put Lucy in the best light.

I wanted to listen and offer encouragement. I also wanted to tell him to ditch her. His eyes were closed, his head leaning against the vinyl siding. Trains crashed past, sometimes stopping and opening their doors, allowing people to come and go. His chest rose and fell under the wool, V-neck sweater that he wore over a white T-shirt. Henry was thin but not too thin, popular in the same way that I was (among the unpopular kids), and was on the debate team, which to me seemed very sexy. I walked a balance beam in that conversation, as with every conversation I had with him about Lucy, between being his friend (and, in theory, hers) and trying to be there for him when their relationship inevitably ended in the way that being "there" meant being "next."

Groups of teenagers like my friends—the leftovers—populate the mastheads of high school newspapers, and thankfully in my case, there were boys in this category. Some of these boys wrote poetry or plays or wore giant cameras slung from their necks, and some joined the debate club or the mock trial team. I was not romantically interested in boys who could write because they were competition. But I was deeply interested in boys who knew the law, boys who could craft a good argument, analytical boys with wire-rimmed glasses, boys who preferred, inexplicably, Holden Caulfield to Jay Gatsby. To me, these boys were all Jay Gatsby, and maybe that was the problem. Maybe my perception of boys (and, later, men) as Gatsbyesque figures of tragedy and longing, in need of the right person, in need of the right hand reaching across the water, was my problem. I didn't want a boy who could write a compelling opening paragraph and who might grow up to enjoy a contented, steady life. I wanted a boy who needed me. A boy who was, somewhere, broken.

# I Was a Good Girlfriend

I met Robb at the door of his mom's car when he handed me a large bird cage with a pale, yellow cockatiel inside. I carried it up the steps of Waterbury Hall, into room 108. I had come to campus a few days early that fall to wear a royal blue polo shirt with the words "Orientation Guide" above my left breast and to welcome new students into our dorm. I helped Robb unload the car, then hesitated before leaving his room. He stood amid his boxed-up and crated CDs, earth-toned clothing, and two electronic keyboards and introduced me to the bird. His hair was too long in the front, and I think I fell in love with him so fast that it seems like it happened even before he told me the bird's name.

"This is Gus."

He majored in elementary education while I studied writing. It should have been a warning sign that he so completely resembled the male characters in my fiction: a sensitive man who loved his mom, a nature lover, quirky, a musician. Within days, we adhered to each other. We put our plastic trays brimming with food next to each other in the dining hall for every meal. We studied together in his room, my room, the library. We kissed and nuzzled in the relative shelter of study rooms and wrote cryptic, sweet notes, sliding them under each other's dorm room doors.

I did all the things that girlfriends of boys do. I wore his oversized shirts. I listened to his music. I got a cockatiel named Gatsby. I got to know his unemployed, keyboard-playing friend, Kris. I brought them bottles of good beer, with the caps already pried off, while they jammed late into the night.

"Girls like me to be their first," he told me one day while we discussed my virgin condition. "What do you think that means?"

I had no idea, but I was ready to join the other girls who had spread apart their knees for this boy. I was a sophomore. I was straight. It was time.

I wore a red dress to a piano recital on a Saturday when his roommate was away. There was a white rose handed to me wrapped in tissue paper, an hour of classical music, and his narrow dorm bed, darkness, and the rubbery smell of latex. The dress was draped across the laddered back of his dorm-issue desk chair. His skin and the hair that covered all the various parts of him were up against me under the shaggy blankets, and when he entered it didn't feel like much. It hurt but not a lot. He just felt big and clunky. He was careful. No fireworks. No bleeding. No reverence. Just getting the job done.

He asked me, when it was over, "Was that okay? Are you okay?"

It took at least three times for us to transition from having sex to making love, and we did it with dedication whenever his roommate went home, which was most weekends. I remember Saturday and Sunday mornings in the dining hall, sitting together, the previous night's activities still on our skin and between our legs, and gazing at each other across an expanse of scrambled eggs, toast, potatoes, and fruit. The night's secrets hung between us, but of course they weren't secrets at all. Other couples, scattered around the dining hall, had that same look of a bad night's sleep on one-half of a small mattress.

Across all the months that turned into years with this boy, and all the months and years that turned into decades with other boys who turned into men, and the miles and nights of sex, I never once stopped to wonder if being with women might be better. I was not struggling to stay straight. I cannot look back and admit to the secret I was carrying because there was no secret, no optical illusion, no trickery.

When his best friend, Mark, married the terrifyingly skinny Estelle, Robb was the best man at their unremarkable ceremony in Syracuse, New York. He wore a gray tuxedo, cut from glossy fabric that was almost reflective, like aluminum foil. I overdressed in a velvet green dress with a crinkly skirt held in a bell shape by under-layers of tulle. We could have been going to a prom. At the reception, I stood obediently among a group of Estelle's friends for the bouquet toss, and the bundle of disarrayed flowers, stems, and ribbons dropped unbidden into my arms. When Mark removed the garter from Estelle's bony thigh (with his teeth, I believe, to a soundtrack of whooping and catcalling) and then tossed it toward the single men, Robb dove for it like a football player. I have a photograph of him sliding that lacy, elastic loop over my knee with Mark and Estelle looking on approvingly. Robb and I spent that night alone in Mark's bachelor apartment and made love ferociously. I was insecure from the day: all those people, his friends, his family, all the expectations and hype about meeting the new girlfriend—and the garter. I needed him inside me as far as he could get, under Mark's blankets, our feet pointing at Mark's giant television, beer cans and wine bottles scattered across the acreage of carpeting. He had spent that day with his old friends, laughing with them, sending me sideways smiles and glances. I knew my role: to be the fun, new girlfriend, to be nothing like the old, weird, moody girlfriend, to try to bond with the paper-thin-new-wife-of-the-best-friend. Even at nineteen, I knew the role, and I played it.

During a semester in London, I carried a photo of Robb in a brick-colored wooden frame. At Trafalgar Square, St. Paul's Cathedral, the Tower Bridge I pulled the photo out and had a friend take a picture of me posing with it. I continued this practice as my two friends and I traveled around Europe for three weeks following the semester. We bought Eurorail passes and carried tattered copies of *Let's Go* and studied train schedules like scripture. France, Switzerland, Spain. We learned to exchange each country's currency for the next and how to ask where the bathroom is in four different languages.

I cried alone in a hostel in Madrid while my friends went to watch a bullfight. Torment and slaughter of an animal seemed like terrible entertainment, and I stayed behind and bought myself a cheap bottle of Spanish wine. Our room was small—just a plain rectangle with three beds and a sink. I stretched out on the scratchy blanket on my bunk and caught up on my journaling, which didn't take long enough. I sat on the floor and tossed playing cards at a trash can, seeing how many I could get to flutter inside. Even then, I was terrible at being alone, and this act of sitting still after weeks of constant motion gave me time to feel homesick. I wrote Robb a longing letter. *I miss you. I want to come home. You are the one.*

When I got home, I developed all the pictures and collected the prints of photos of Robb into an album of "our trip through Europe." When I think now about the sweetness of that, the memory of those 5x7 prints glued into a scrapbook with captions identifying each significant European location written in black Sharpie, I am struck by how sincere I was and how little I received in return and the fact that I knew it at the time: I would give disproportionately to what I received because it's what good girlfriends do. When I gave him the album, in candlelight, he didn't speak. He just turned each page, smiling.

I had been back for a couple of weeks, at my parents' house in Portland, Maine, waiting for Robb to finish his semester, before I saw him. We had somehow convinced my parents to let him live in their guest room for the summer with the following conditions: he had to get a job, he had to pay rent, and I was never to be caught in the guest room with him. That's what happened: I never got caught.

Robb took a Greyhound from Syracuse to Boston, where my brother picked him up and gave him a ride to Portland. I waited for them on that early June day in shorts and bare feet in the back of my parents' car with the hatchback up. I wanted to see the moment that my brother's pickup made the turn into the driveway. I wanted my eyes to meet Robb's. I wanted a picture. I sat, coiled like a spring, listening to Paul McCartney sing "Maybe I'm Amazed" on an infinitely repeating loop. I kept my camera balanced on my knee for a half hour so I would be ready to capture the moment. In that picture, my brother's Ford Ranger is midway through a sharp swing into the driveway and the windshield reflects only white sky and light. Robb is not visible through the glass. My memory of not seeing him in that moment is clearer than what he looked like when he stepped out of the truck.

"What would you say if I asked you to marry me?"

Robb had been in Maine only for a few days. We were away together for the weekend. He had finished looking at the photo album, and we were naked, wrapped in blankets. His head was in my lap.

"I would say yes, of course." I stroked his hair.

The next thing I remember is that he was on the phone, announcing our engagement to his mother. I remember trying to squelch my own shock, trying to re-cast the story even as it unfolded so that it looked less like I had been tricked. Still wrapped in a sheet, I called my parents with the news.

## After Tall Probably Gay Steve, Third Steve I Didn't Love Back, and a Marc

I decided not to marry Robb. Our mismatched-ness became too glaring. I had read just enough Butler and Faludi to know that it was not my job to buy his beer and make meals for his sketchy guitar-player friend. The charm of letting him put another keyboard and then another electronic music component on my credit card wore thin the day we were arguing over money, and he said to me, "You can't make me pay my own bills."

I moved through three Steves, and I was barely out of the confusing woods of rebounding from Marc when I met Jay in a freezing rainstorm on a sandy beach in Portland, Maine's, East End. Driving home from somewhere, I had stopped at the beach to take my dog for a walk before holing up inside for the evening with dry socks and hot tea. The beach was deserted. Icy rain sleeted sideways across the shoreline, but one figure trudged along the high tide mark. Hunched like a turtle and silhouetted in the diminished light, he was trailed by two dogs.

His eyes met mine through the thick sleet, and he told me his name and that he was in the phone book. I called him. For the next several months, we made giggling, meaningful eye contact from behind midday mugs of foaming cappuccino and over steaming plates of spicy Thai noodles and slices of lime. The seed of our affair germinated in the flexibility of my graduate school schedule and took root in his seeming lack of responsibilities beyond attending multiple twelve-step meetings every day. It unfolded its leaves in weekday mornings spent sleeping late in his expensive bedding, then walking the dogs before I hit the library for the day.

I can still say, all these years later, that he was the most objectively attractive man I was ever with. Jay had a comic book superhero angularity to his jawline and a way of squinting when he gazed into the distance, evoking heroic, young sea captains. And he was huge in the best way. His expensive flannel shirts fell all the way to my knees, and I had to roll the sleeves up halfway just to expose my hands while I made coffee in his apartment. For this man, I became addicted to cigarettes. I had no idea that what felt good was not always good.

I had just landed my first professional job and believed I was on my way somewhere when Jay announced, in my own kitchen, that it was time for him to move on. "That friend of yours. That guy, John. The artist," he counseled. "You should be with that guy."

"Fuck you." I paced furiously across the threshold from kitchen to bedroom and back.

"No, I'm serious," he said, carefully using only I statements. "I think someone like that is better for you." He held up his hands, palms facing me. He said something like, "But that's really your lane, not mine," or some other twelve-step-inspired pseudo-insightful sloganesque phrase meant to make what was about to happen to me my own fault.

I was not shocked that our relationship was ending. I had determined weeks ago that I loved him but in the way one might love an all-expenses-paid surprise trip for one to a tiny, remote island in the Caribbean. He was beautiful, and I was having a lot of fun, but there wasn't ultimately a lot to do there. What shocked me was that it was him, not me, who reached the end first.

"I think it's time for you to leave," I said, trying to resume control. And he did. He rose from the stool made of blond wood, walked away from my tall kitchen table, threaded his way through the three rooms that composed my apartment, and was gone. An hour later, I called John.

The question here isn't whether John was expecting the call or how Jay knew that John was the right next man. The question here is why I was so lousy at being alone. The question is why I didn't, at this moment when my professional life was blooming like a lily and when I had a garden apartment near the ocean, take a year or a month or even a weekend to figure out how to be alone.

It doesn't matter now.

# We Are All at the Edge

Felix Baumgartner knows how to take a fall. The first human being to break the sound barrier in a skydive, he led a team funded by Red Bull (manufacturer of weird little caffeine drinks) and designed a specialized balloon that lifted his specialized capsule twenty-four miles above the New Mexico desert, where the sky transitions into space. During his dive, he reached 834 miles per hour. He hit the ground before his own screams.

This achievement took more than one attempt. Baumgartner's first jump was scrapped due to high winds. I streamed the video feed from the safety of my desk. I answered emails and took calls while Baumgartner waited for hours, shrunk to a small rectangle in the corner of my monitor, while his team worked to determine if this was to be the day. He took the news with grace: no launch today. He winced a small smile at the webcam.

Consulting for the Red Bull team was Joseph Kittinger, the former record holder in the world of crazy-ass skydiving. Kittinger's most famous jump brought his body to a speed of 614 miles per hour. That's woefully short of the 760-mile-per-hour speed of conversations, babies crying, and car horns. In the moments after the decision to scrap Baumgartner's jump, Kittinger seemed overcome with disappointment. He sat in a mission-control-like room, lips pressed together, head haloed by giant headphones, elbows on the desk. His hands were clasped, fingers gnarled and held up as if in prayer to the deities of frustration.

One of the commentators remarked that during a twenty-four-mile skydive, one of the hardest things to do is wait. The jumper must let five long minutes pass before pulling the rip cord. His mind will tell him after just two or three minutes that it's already been too long. He will want to do what must come naturally to a skydiver: deploy the parachute. While he wondered if his blood was heating up from the pressure or if his limbs were about to freeze from exposure, Baumgartner had to wait. Wait while he approached and then passed through the earth's cloud cover. Wait while the quilt of the American Southwest enlarged to become just one brown square. Wait while his parents, on their first trip to America, shielded their eyes with their hands, watching their son grow from a dot in the sky to a man on the ground. While they waited on Earth, he waited too. Families wait and then fall together.

As I'm falling asleep at night, sometimes my brain conjures the edges of cliffs, and I am jerked awake. In these dream states, I imagine edging the toes of my boots at the place where the earth falls away, and that dizziness kicks me upright, where I sit breathing hard, groping for something familiar. The dark of our bedroom compounds the disorientation. In the first year of our cohabitation, Kara and I struggled over my need for a nightlight. She thought it was intrusive, and she eventually won. We sleep with no light. I miss the data it provides when the cliff shakes me awake.

There's a variation on the visions I have of falling. In this one, my kids play on wet, stony ground. They run and laugh, chasing each other, playing tag. And as I lie there, trying to sleep with this pervasive film unfolding in my head, one of my kids (it's always Owen, my youngest) steps too close to the edge and falls. It takes a fraction of a moment. He's there, then he's gone. I wish my brain didn't joust with me this way, that it didn't jam this sharp-as-an-icepick image into being so often. I'm not asleep when it happens. This is not a dream as much as it is a private movie that plays when I'm on the edge of sleep. Owen falls. The scene freezes because there's that chilling knowledge that he's gone sent clicking into place. Sometimes I roll over in bed, open my eyes, and focus on the green glow of the clock radio in an effort to redirect my brain. But it persists. This moment, the moment right after my youngest child has plummeted hundreds of feet, either bashed against the cliff's face or drowned, stages itself on repeat in my imagination. There are variations of this. Sometimes I have time to lunge for him as he steps off the precipice, and we fall together, but first we hang there in the air, in a road-runner-like freeze, for just a breath, and then we fall. This vision never stops with the moment of the fall—it continues into the part where Kara and I look at each other with the gravity of all the loss in the world, and she pivots on her heel and runs to find help, leaving me screaming my son's name into the mist, craning to see down the angry face of this island. I sit up, rearrange my pillows, lie down again, pull the quilt closer to my face, wait to see if this waking nightmare is still there. If it is, this all starts over.

It must be something about edges. Something about living on them, testing them, nudging them with the toe of a boot to see how they respond. Edges are border lands, where the culture of salt water comes up hard against that of cold stone while sky and wind mingle with tenacious, spindly grasses and scrubby flowers. In between, terns and gulls find crevices and rocky shelves on which to build their homes. On stormy days, they must lose sons and daughters in the abyss.

On October 14, 2012, I left my house and drove four miles to my office, where the internet was faster, to watch Felix Baumgartner's jump live online on the sixty-fifth anniversary of the day Chuck Yeager first broke the sound barrier in a machine that was part airplane, part rocket. I don't know why I needed to see this twenty-four-mile freefall. Maybe it was a need to see someone face that kind of abyss, step into it, and survive. Gravity would pull him through darkness to light, from the abstract of space to the concrete of the land.

It was a Sunday. We were home, Kara and I. New to her home, I was barely unpacked. I was supposed to think of it as our home, no longer just her home, but it would take years for all of my things to make it out of boxes. I had left my former home like a refugee, abandoning years' worth of belongings. I took what I needed: my clothes, favorite mixing bowls and coffee mugs, half of the framed photos of the kids, books, both hard-covered dictionaries, photo albums, including the one with the wedding photos. Two of the green-and-white-striped chairs from the patio set. I didn't bring the other four chairs or the matching umbrella. I didn't bring the Electrolux I found at a yard sale or the espresso maker we brought back from Italy. I didn't bring a single thing from the storage shed behind the house—the building where we stuck the things we didn't know what to do with. Years later, my ex and I would take a Saturday and clean the whole building of my possessions. We rented a dumpster, and I disposed of college papers, a broken word processor, and my high school prom dress. I threw that pink, fluffy, satiny dress into the depths of the green dumpster. It rained that night, and I sat in bed thinking of raindrops ruining the white flocked flowers imprinted on the pink satin. Things were always cracking inside me.

That Sunday, there in what still felt like Kara's living room, I picked up my car keys and extracted myself from the sunny comfort. My kids were not there. I felt their absence like a gaping abyss, like I was missing an arm or a lung. Kara didn't understand why I needed to leave our midmorning, Sunday routine of coffee and NPR. Neither did I, but I left, drove to my office, and sat in my purple office chair to watch someone else's son fall.

Baumgartner was dressed like an astronaut with full-on space gear, as if for a moon walk. His capsule looked like the one from the scene in *Apollo 13* when the craft plops into the ocean. It was a six-sided, faceted, white jewel with small, thick windows and sides adorned with decals: his name, yellow-and-black hazard stripes, Red Bull. Baumgartner strode from his Airstream trailer, as much as one can stride in a spacesuit, then was strapped into the capsule. A giant helium balloon delivered him to almost marathon-height above the earth. A cam attached to a capsule outrigger showed his unsteady steps onto the jump platform, and another one broadcast the view from over his shoulder. Wrapping his thickly gloved hands around one padded thing at a time, he maneuvered his legs into place. He moved like he was encased in lead. He faced the dark of space and the distant curve of our home planet, hovering in the place where atmosphere meets the void, where air is far below, and where he might have traded life for death. He saluted and stepped off.

It was like my waking nightmares, but with no option to jerk into wakefulness. Whatever Baumgartner was feeling was on direct feed from reality, not some tortured imaginings from which he could rouse himself. He just had to fall. His parents stood below, in the desert, waiting for their son to appear in the sky, and I wondered if they too had suffered from visions like mine.

He fell for almost four and a half minutes before pulling the cord. For a time, his body spun, and he said later he was afraid he might lose consciousness, but he held onto awareness and somehow controlled the spin. He said later that he didn't even hear the sonic boom because he was too busy trying to steady his whirling body. The boom happens when air can't get out of the way fast enough, and what we hear is the cone-shaped shock wave.

From below, he looked like an action figure—G.I. Joe or Buzz Lightyear—plummeting from a toy capsule. The footage switched to a vantage point of a helicopter that met him at the landing site. He drifted toward the red, desert ground, and when his feet touched, the momentum carried him forward three steps, and he looked fully alive and athletic, not like the barely-able-to-lift-his-own-legs version that had eased itself onto the jump platform. Back in the realm of gravity, life returned to his limbs, and he raised his arms in triumph. Falling, with parachute deployed, is both surrendering to and resisting gravity. He controlled the fall. He landed. Records were broken. Even when we land safely, and in the right spot, things get broken when we fall.

# Provincetown I

My boyfriend John and I ate vegetarian sandwiches high on a second-story deck of a café in Provincetown, Massachusetts, watching drag queens thread their way through crowds of chunky, short-haired lesbians. It was my first trip to Provincetown. On the sidewalk below the café, a very tall, muscular Black woman wearing a sequined, legless bodysuit, a feathered, orange headdress, and blocky high heels stalked the asphalt. She handed out glossy postcards advertising her show with nails so long it looked difficult to slide each card off the top of the pile. Everything about her was practiced and artful. Holding each card delicately between thumb and forefinger, she served them up with flirtatious eye contact and teasing remarks. Muscled, broad shoulders and exposed thick arms bugled joyous exposure in the sun. Eyelashes almost as long as her fingernails fanned her cheeks like the wings of a resting butterfly. Her voice, baritone and oaky but also feminine and melodic, drifted up to us on the balcony. She called men and women "Honey" as she touched them lightly with her daggered fingertips. She had on more makeup that day than the entirety of all the makeup I had worn in my life. She was the first drag queen I had ever seen.

I leaned against the railing of the balcony and closed my eyes, feeling the sun on my cheeks and forehead. The babble of tourists, shuffling of feet, and the queen's teasing, flirting voice wrapped me in a soothing din. The sound of pencil lead against toothy paper brushed itself into the soundtrack, and I knew that John was sketching. My eyes eased open, and I watched the parade of people, their fingers interlaced with those of their lovers. A short woman with lustrous black hair pulled into a ponytail held hands with a stocky woman with a buzz cut and a rat tail while they window shopped for T-shirts. A slim man in low-riding jeans leaned his back against the bricks of a storefront while his bulky, motorcycle-guy boyfriend whispered into his ear. The slim man giggled. Every muscle in his body seemed buttery. Two men with wire-rimmed glasses and stomachs bulging under their polo shirts shuffled by, holding hands.

Provincetown was a place for lovers. And blessed as I was with the life of a straight thirtysomething, I assumed all these people were out. To the extent that I bothered to think about it at all, I assumed that they acted this way in their own hometowns—that they held hands and kissed in public wherever they went. My worldview resembled a genetic chart from high school biology, as if "gay" and "out" were two recessive genes that could combine to form this particular, immutable quality. Further, and I cringe to admit this now, my narrow reflections carried a "good for them" quality—the kind that would include a playful punch to someone's shoulder. "Bully for you." It's possible to admire the swirling beauty of a goldfish without noticing the confines of the bowl. It took years for me to develop awareness of the bowl I was in and to re-cast my notions as something resembling real life. When my heart and membership to the straight world were stolen by a woman, I had to readjust my vision to see the curving glass all around me. But that all came later.

John and I finished our sandwiches and joined the parade of people. He slipped his hand into mine and gave my fingers a squeeze. It did not occur to me to plug us both into the place on the grid where "straight" and "out" intersected. It didn't cross my young, privileged mind that those two qualities automatically coexist. Always. The slanted afternoon sunlight beat down, lighting and warming me. I continued my people watching, checking out a woman in her twenties with clipped black hair, laughing while she told a story to her girlfriend. Her fingers were wrapped around a paper coffee cup, and she gestured wildly as she made her point. The girlfriend, whose ponytail was threaded through the back of a baseball cap, smiled as she listened. She had her fingertips hooked into the pocket of her partner's jeans, and they rode there as the pair made their way through the crowd. She was gay. She was out. Good for her.

John and I stayed at a bed and breakfast run by a straight couple in a town down the road from Provincetown. Sitting by a fire pit in their front yard, sharing a bottle of wine, John and I fantasized about moving to the Cape and starting a B&B. This is what our hosts had done, and we toasted their good decision. John clinked his glass against mine, his trimmed beard and round glasses becoming less visible as the night grew closer. He was a painter, and I knew he was paying attention to the dying light, how it lit only the rims of the brick buildings and backlit the leaves, deepening the colors.

Several miles away, on the highway, cars with rainbow bumper stickers streamed steadily past on their way to Provincetown. I imagined that in the safe darkness of cars, male fingers wrapped around male fingers and female fingers played with hair at the napes of women's necks. Beyond the highway, the grasses that fringed the dunes changed colors. Cape Cod breezes, made delicious by salt, blew across us as we talked into the night. With my feet propped against the rocks that bordered the fire pit, I drank wine with the man I would eventually marry and then later divorce.

Married or divorced. Together or apart. In love or out of love. These dichotomies all proved false over the next decade. My assumptions had to adapt into realities, had to take on dimensions, had to shift like Cape Cod light on a summer evening. It was like that trick of taking a two-sided strip of paper, twisting it in the middle, then taping one end to the other: that which used to have two sides now has only one.

# Not Not a Tenant

In 1996 I rode in a friend's Subaru while we crawled across the width of New Hampshire in a brutal snowstorm, trying to take ourselves skiing in Vermont. The last thing I remember about that night is a conversation about how unsafe the driving conditions had become and an agreement that we should stop at the next hotel. The next memory is of an argument I had with a morphine button in the hospital, and the next one after that is of using a walker to get to and from the bathroom.

And that's how I came into enough money to pay off my student loans, take my family on a vacation in the Florida Keys, buy a new couch, and make a modest down payment on a house. These were the door prizes that my lawyer extracted from an insurance company, and they were intended as redress for the pain and suffering involved in recovering from twelve broken ribs, a cracked skull, and a crushed pelvis. It was not enough—nothing can ever be enough to compensate for the many years of clinical treatment for PTSD, the forever pain in my lower back that would sometimes cripple me, and all the Xanax required to get me into a car for the next decade and a half.

But since I had the money, I wanted a house. John and I shopped for a house together, even though it was to be my house that he lived in, not quite as a tenant but not *not* a tenant either. We looked at houses across the fifteen-mile stretch between Pembroke and Eastport and all side roads along the way. Sometimes his parents trailed along to help John shop for my house.

We looked at a house that his parents loved: a small apartment atop a storefront in Eastport. His parents were thrilled that, if this were my house, John could open a gallery on the first floor. The living quarters were cute and brightly colored with gently sloping floors and funky, painted windowsills. But as I imagined the two of us living there, perhaps someday with a child, the adorably small bedroom seemed less adorable.

John was attracted to fixer uppers that I believed we had no hope of fixer-uppering. Sagging foundations, aged wiring, crumbled chimneys, and hopelessly thin, leaking window glass—he loved all that stuff. I too wanted something we could leave a mark on, make our own, but I was afraid of the big, ugly repairs: foundations, roofs, electrical systems, plumbing. He seemed unafraid. I was the opposite. There were things I needed in a house. I needed to know I could meet its needs. I needed room to grow a family. I needed a lilac tree. It didn't seem too much to ask. Where was my agency? Like a quantum particle, I occupied two spaces: the sphere of the strong, feminist woman and also that of the good girlfriend. These personas floated like planets in neighboring orbits that could wave to each other but never touch.

We looked at a Victorian-style home with questionable neighbors in Eastport. It had perfectly appointed everythings: the floors were level and made of shining hardwood; glossy, asparagus-colored tiles framed the fireplace in the parlor; and the kitchen cabinetry enjoyed levelness and square corners. We took my family into that one, my parents and my visiting brother and sister-in-law. We also showed them a much older house in a nicer part of town. It had ancient wiring, rings from water damage on most of the ceilings, and warped, brown paneling in the living room. Only halfway through the Victorian, my sister-in-law met my eye and said in her trademark, incredulous tone, "There's no contest here." John hated the Victorian. I pressed him, once we were alone, for the reason. "I don't know. It's just too clean."

There was a house we viewed over and over. It was unfinished—unlivable—and the owner gave us a key. A two-story former sea captain's house that had been radically rebuilt by a Canadian man hoping to retire in it, I could never entirely stop thinking about it. It was firmly in the fixer-upper category, but it had a new roof, new furnace, new wiring, windows, triple-flue chimney, and had been gutted during the renovation. Whatever fixtures were to be installed in the bathroom or kitchen would be brand new.

The house had additions off two sides of the rectangular living room. These extra rooms came to be called "the big sunroom" and "the small sunroom." The big one was the length of the house and just twelve feet wide or so. Its long wall was a bank of windows overlooking nothing but the ugly trailer next door. The ceiling was made of rough two-by-eights, and the windows on one of the narrow ends were blocked almost entirely by the only lilac tree on the property. It was visible from the small sunroom too, as the two rooms shared one corner of the house. The small sunroom was semi-circular—formed with multiple surfaces, like a pentagon, like a geometry lesson. The sheet-rocked ceiling in the small sunroom was cathedral-style and came to a point where the carpenter had apparently given up, having no idea how to join the sections neatly. A bare lightbulb dangled from an exposed wire at the ceiling's peak.

In the large sunroom, the owner had left two mint-colored rocking chairs. At the end of many workdays, I let myself into this house and sat in one of those two chairs, looking out the bank of windows, imagining what the view could be if the trailer were gone, or at least hidden by a tall fence or creative landscaping. Sometimes John went with me and sat in the other chair. The sun filled the room, the rocking chairs cast shadows on the plywood subflooring, and we imagined ourselves moving in and finishing the place off. There were other houses requiring less work, but in the end, it was a compromise—as so many things in marriage are, though we were not married. I wanted him to stay. He wanted to want to stay. He could not imagine himself in the slick finish of the Victorian that needed no work just as I could not fathom moving into a house that immediately needed to be rebuilt. This house needed our help but would keep us safe and dry in the meantime. We could hang curtains over the doors and live on subfloors until we could do more, and we could live knowing that the roof was solid and the wiring would not spark a fire and kill us in the night. This is the house I purchased. We kept the rocking chairs, painted the subfloors, and lit fires in the wood stove I bought for the living room.

Ancient Celtic people, known for their knots, are credited in some texts with giving us the phrase "tying the knot." In the pre-Christian tradition of handfasting, a couple's hands were tied together with cord or ribbon, though this rite was a symbol of engagement not marriage. In the late 1700s, someone got a rumor started that handfasting, combined with a ceremony in which all the verbs tantalized with future tense (i.e., "I will take this man"), granted a couple a 366-day period in which to try each other out. People mistakenly believed, for many years, that the church would overlook sex between members of an unwed couple for one year, and if there were no children at the year's end, the couple could part ways without angering God or anyone else. This isn't true at all, but I like the idea that people could tie the knot, but not too tight, then tie it for real if they wanted to. By buying a house together and starting a life, this is essentially what John and I did.

Sailors and rock climbers will tell you, though, that if your life depends on a knot, you'd best know what you're doing when you tie it because there are a lot of tangled ropes that only look like knots.

# Untying the Knot

In June 2016 physicists, mathematicians, philosophers, and others gathered in Waterloo, Canada, to debate what time is like, how it got started, and what it means when it goes by. The stated goal of the Time in Cosmology conference was "to discuss key questions in early universe cosmology in the light of the question as to whether time is fundamental or emergent." In other words, is time an essential quality or is it fleeting? Is time the length of a day (predictable, constructed) or more like its temperature (unpredictable, capricious)? The conference ended without participants reaching consensus, which makes one wonder how they knew when it was time to leave for the airport.

I want to have a narrative about why we got divorced. I want that time to be describable—something I can pin to a calendar or chart on a graph—but that's not how marriages work. I could blame it on the emotional affair he had. I could blame it on the obvious: that I turned out to be gay. He could blame it on my affair. I could blame it on our differing priorities. I could blame it on money. I could say we never really were in love in the first place and that the babies were all I wanted. I could say he was lazy, and he could say I was a nagging bitch with a rage problem. He could say that I was an active alcoholic. He could say that I was dangerously unpredictable. We could say all those things, and we have, and we were both wrong and both right because most things in marriage are true and false at the same time.

Unlike Robb and Marc and Jay, though, my failed relationship with John will never end even after both of us are buried because we had kids.

Our limited verb tenses can't express what the physicists say: that time and space are more alike than different. My present is here, and my past is next to me, just as I am in the living room and my dog is in the kitchen. Time is a three-dimensional box. Run and ran, type and typed, eat and ate, love and loved, losing and lost all float in proximity to each other in this block theory of time. If it weren't so dark in the box, they could see each other, and we would encounter our past selves so often it wouldn't even seem weird, which is why I feel like I never left my old life when I entered this new one and like my new life was a place I already knew when I got here.

Years after all this happened, during a late-night trip in Portland, Maine, with my fifteen-year-old daughter, I would steer my car into a hotel parking lot and notice a pair of glowing, yellow loops floating overhead in the fog. It was the logo of Infinity Credit Union, next to the hotel, and because my head was already full of thoughts about time as an infinitely large box that goes on forever, the logo made me glance at my daughter and see her as a shimmering hologram—something that would never have happened if I had lived only one, linear life.

# PART 2

# The Love Poetry of Food

In 1971 revered social anthropologist Mary Douglas wrote, "The rules of the menu are not in themselves more or less trivial than the rules of verse to which a poet submits." In her piece "Deciphering a Meal," which some would later call her seminal work, Douglas posited that humans use meals as a code to express qualities of social relationships, such as hierarchy and intimacy. Douglas was a food codebreaker, exploring the grammar of meals, each aspect serving as a part of speech. When is the meal eaten? Where? With whom? How many sides? On what table? With what sort of napkins?

There's a dictionary's-worth of unspoken intentions communicated when we invite a new friend to join us for a meal. Is the relationship dinner-worthy or should we just grab lunch? If it's to be lunch, will it be sit-down or take-out? Do we work together? Are you my boss? If we're having dinner, am I inviting you inside my house or is it too soon for that? Maybe it's better to have a cookout until we know each other better. Or what if you pick up a pizza on your way over? Do I pay you back? Are we splitting it? Do we know each other well enough that I can ask you to grab a bag of ice while you're at the store?

New England winters are long, dark giants that lumber across the geography, casting lonely shadows across our homes and lives. In winter we assemble soups to eat with sourdough made with starter we've kept alive for months. We toss beets and carrots with olive oil and roast them on pans. We stir and season pots of steaming noodles, eat a lot of cheese, drink too much coffee, and watch the horizon for the light to return. Sometimes someone hosts a potluck so we can do these things as a group.

Our friend Georgie held monthly, themed potlucks across these difficult winters, each one offering an opportunity to crack open an international cookbook and order exotic ingredients and spices from the internet. Indian, Japanese, Middle Eastern, Mexican. Platters and hot bowls and casserole dishes arrived in her kitchen wrapped in towels to protect them from the cold, and everyone placed these offerings on the table before emerging from layers of downy coats and soft hats and mittens. Georgie's kitchen woodstove glowed from its corner, and we smiled huge smiles at each other, hugging the people we knew the best or signaling nice-to-meet-you nods at the new people.

We caught up on our what-have-you-been-up-to's and how-is-your-woodpile-holding-up's, standing with plates of curry or hot peppers or fried eels or noodle soups. There was always drinking and laughter. Outside, cars packed the dooryard, squeezed in between snow banks and shoveled paths, between the barn and the house and the woodshed. When the first guests wanted to leave, the last guests had to jockey cars around in the dark to let them maneuver out.

Georgie introduced me to Kara. New to the area. Here for an internship. She seemed aloof—someone who viewed us all, and this region, like a social scientist. Like she might like to pin us to cardboard affixed with neatly typed labels. In this area, we had plenty of people like this: people who passed through. People who tried us out, then realized just how *far* we really were from restaurants and bookstores and galleries, and then fled. I don't remember what she wore that night, but I picture her in a hippie-style headscarf, determinedly dated eyeglasses, and the tie-dyed, three-quarter-sleeve pullover shirt she often wears now. She for sure wore jeans, hiking boots, and wool socks she had knitted herself, but whatever she wore, I appraised her as someone who would never stay here.

"The two major contrasted food categories are meals versus drinks," wrote Douglas. "Meals properly require the use of at least one mouth-entering utensil per head, whereas drinks are limited to mouth-touching ones." Inviting someone over for drinks, she goes on to say, is less structured than sharing a meal and is also less intimate. We can have drinks with almost anyone, but we reserve social meals for those we know the best. It's a distinction between what enters us and what just touches us.

I always drank too much at Georgie's parties. Always. In the presence of a collection of wine bottles and nobody counting my drinks, I had too many. My drinking that night is both a point on a linear timeline and a dot in the pointillist backdrop that became a foreground in my later life. But on that night, before I went home in the darkness with my husband and young daughter, I had written Kara a note prompted, I'm sure, by some joke that made us laugh together for what was probably the first time. I had scrawled "I.O.U. one million dollars" on a piece of scrap paper from Georgie's kitchen. Somehow I had staggered into Kara's debt. Today we sometimes laugh that I am still working it off.

Debt, it turns out, is a normal part of social eating. We invested heavily in these meals, often spending hours squinting at recipes, measuring powdered sumac or whole cumin seeds or other spices we had never used before. These investments were both offerings and invitations: take what I have made for you and spend time with me. On Indian night, a woman named Nancy arrived with a platter of elaborately arranged toppings: chopped peanuts, scallions, coconut, mint leaves, lime pickles. I've seen this expression of love referred to as an "inconvenience display." See how long I spent on this: it's for you. I have not forgotten how finely she chopped the glistening mango. When Kara and I make curry with toppings, even today, I think of it as a gift.

# Closer to Fine

It was ladies' night at Georgie's. I had no business showing up with a guitar—no real skills yet to justify carrying that instrument case—but it made me feel cool, so I brought it anyway. The screen door banged shut behind me after I wrestled my instrument into the house. Carrying the guitar around made me feel some hope of connection. Like the case might carry more than just the guitar I could barely play.

Kara showed up with a guitar too and took me more seriously than I had ever taken myself. She sat in a chair, her instrument across her lap, delicately picking her way across some melody. Sheepish about my drunken indebtedness, I sat near her, listening to her play while she listened to someone talking. She is a good listener.

Later, she turned to me and nodded her chin toward my guitar case, leaning against a door frame across the room. "Is that yours?"

I nodded, feeling called on a bluff.

"Well break it out, then."

The first song we ever sang together was Dar Williams's "Iowa."

I knew the chord shapes, and she taught me what order to play them in. With the tips of her long, brown hair brushing against her forearm, she leaned over and watched me switch from G to C and back again. She reached over and touched my forefinger and said, "Lift this one and hammer it back down." And I did. And it sounded good.

In my memory, Kara and I became the center of that party, though I'm skeptical now when I wonder whether that was true for anyone other than me. She knew the songs I knew. She found harmonies to my melodies. We took requests. People sang along. The room was warm, people's faces were flushed with wine and heat, and they sang. I had known nothing like this before. It felt like what I had imagined playing music could be. John had joined a band, at my urging, to find a way to connect with more people socially, and his devotion to their weekly practices quickly spilled into the rest of our lives like a river flooding its banks. It had become a source of arguments in which we used accusations like weaponry against each other. I had not found my way to forgiving him for coldly walking out on me every Tuesday night, but if I had known that it could feel like this, I would have forgiven him sooner. That's the same night that Kara taught me to play "Closer to Fine" by the Indigo Girls.

Over many years, these songs became parts of our story on par with vows, rings, and anniversaries. They morphed into foundational qualities, like the bricks in our house or the fact of the ocean. Many years later, we would take both of my kids to a Dar Williams concert at the Stone Mountain Arts Center in western Maine, where my son would fall asleep leaning against my arm and my daughter would breathlessly get an autograph. Many years later, Kara and I would attend an Indigo Girls concert at the same venue just hours after getting married on a beach on Cape Cod. Many years later, on our tenth wedding anniversary, the Indigo Girls would be playing a concert in New Jersey with Dar Williams, and we would decide not to go because it was just too far, but the temptation would be palpable just because what are the odds of that happening?

Above the house, while we played, stars drilled their way through the dark and appeared like shining pinpoints of hope above our heads. I couldn't see them. Not yet. But wherever "fine" was, I moved closer to it that night.

# Things You Don't Know

Imagine that you are a thirty-eight-year-old woman and the primary breadwinner in your house. You are the mom of two kids, ages three and one. In addition to your jobs as Mom and Primary Breadwinner, you serve as Dinner Maker, Social Secretary, Household Administrator, and Head Shopper. Your marriage is a rickety house built on spindly stilts straddling a fault line in an earthquake hazard zone, so sometimes you think you might be working for FEMA, but you're not issued a hardhat.

You and your husband fight. You fight about money. You fight about vacuuming. You fight about laundry. Snow shoveling. Groceries. Child care. Vacation plans. Holidays. You decide to join a band together, but he leaves you out, so you fight about that. He accuses you of having anger issues, so you fight about that. You accuse him of emotional infidelity with a friend, so you fight about that. He accuses you of being someone who likes fighting, so you fight about that. The rickety house teeters and yaws over a chasm widening beneath its frail frame. You know you might all tumble into the gaping abyss, and you care less every day.

But imagine that all this ridiculous drama is a symptom and not the disease afflicting your marriage. You read so much feminist writing assuring you it wouldn't be like this that your own expectations have become the termites drilling through the wooden braces that hold your house aloft. You are sure you ordered the everything bagel of feminism topped with career fulfillment, skillful attachment parenting, a kitchen filled with organic whole foods, ample free time, and a vibrant social life. You are certain that if you're not having it all it's because someone's doing something wrong. The two of you are fighting over all the things you're fighting over, but really you're fighting over the failure of your life to measure up to what you think you were promised by the great feminist thinkers and activists who had sworn to liberate you. They couldn't. They didn't.

You are working full-time, nursing babies, pumping breast milk in your office, sleep-deprived, sick of the grocery store and the infinite schlepping of ingredients to and from the car, and so weary of the world that when planes fly into the World Trade Center on September 11, it just deepens a numbness that is already there. One night, when baby number two is less than a year old, and you have returned to full-time work at the domestic violence agency even though you have not slept through the night for three years, you are driving home from work in the dark of winter. Your body is so tired that every cell cries for relief, and your eyelids threaten to close over and over across your thirty-minute commute north across the rural highway. Through force of will, you make it to the mouth of your driveway—but not the extra two hundred feet to the house—before falling asleep. When you wake up fifteen minutes later, with the car still running, you have this thought: *I'm going to die.*

Years later, you will tell a therapist you're pretty sure this is when your drinking got out of control.

In the middle of that mess, you bring your guitar to a potluck dinner, and you're not sure why. You know there's no way you're going to lead a singalong or otherwise perform in front of people, so you have no explanation for why you wrestled your instrument case through the doors of your house, your car, and Georgie's house. But sure enough you end up playing with someone who seems to think you *are* good enough to be included, or at least you're not so terrible you need to be excluded. This idea—that you're not terrible—feels like a drink of water after crawling miles through the desert, and you want to feel that way again, so you email her something like, "Maybe we could get together to play music again some time." You might have said, "That was really fun. I'd love to have that experience again." You certainly did *not* say, "I'm dying of loneliness in my marriage, and I wonder if you might be something I could have all for myself."

She responds with something like, "Sure." Years later, you recognize that lackluster response for the guarded enthusiasm that it was.

So you arrive at her house on your way home from work one day, and she burns the sweet potato quesadillas she makes you for dinner. Years later, you know that she has a habit of putting food on the stove and trying to use the cook time to get some other chore done. Years later, you will find yourself frequently turning down the flame under the pan when she's cooking to give the food a fighting chance.

But that night you don't care that the tortillas are blackened because nobody has made you dinner for years. At her table, while you're both picking off the burned parts, you're laughing about it. You're also talking about books and world events and ideas, which is refreshing because most conversations you have with your friends now are about breastfeeding, co-sleeping, and the universal habits of husbands; while you need those conversations and love those friends, you have forgotten that you have a whole other depth of experience to offer. Like you, she has a master's degree and a full-time job in her field. Like you, she's really into her dog and reads a lot of books. Unlike you, she's not married, not a mom, and has enviable self-confidence.

You have brought your little pile of songs with you, sheets of lyrics with chords written over them, and after dinner the two of you awkwardly play together in her living room, and then you drive home. This happens a few times before you decide to make it a weekly commitment. You have learned the harmony to about three songs before you realize you're probably calling her too often, emailing her too much, and referring to her in conversation with other people too frequently.

THINGS YOU KNOW

1. You are lonely.
2. Your loneliness is your husband's fault.
3. You are irrevocably straight.

THINGS YOU DON'T KNOW

1. Things are about to get complicated.
2. Items 2 and 3 are false.

# Pulling Out the Stops

She talked to me about books. About sentences. She laughed at my jokes. She teased me for my shortcomings instead of being afraid of them. She made vegetarian dinners, and her house was always a glowing, orderly place. Sticks of maple and birch filled the firewood bin, lap quilts were folded neatly on the backs of couches and chairs, books filled the bookcases. The path to her back door was precision-shoveled—the interior walls formed by the blade of her snow shovel were military-straight. She had a hand-lettered sign in her bedroom (now our bedroom) that read, in rainbow colors, "Gratitude. Intention." Kara's love for me was picked up by my receivers as a sharp insight into who I really was, a refusal to be intimidated, and smiling, teasing affirmation.

We were both nonprofit professionals. Kara worked at an education-focused organization with a sprawling mission. She was the program director and spent her time creating art camps, a birding festival, pottery and music lessons, and other experiences designed to foster community wellness. I was assistant director at a domestic violence agency where I managed the emergency shelter, responded to hotline calls, liaised with the police, and gritted my teeth watching systems grind women down into complacent, terrified versions of themselves when all they wanted was safety. My work was bone-crushing and hers seemed fun. My work was slowly turning up the heat on my natural cynicism while her work seemed to uplift her hope. Regardless, she made food, I ate. She talked, I listened. She cleaned up the dishes, I let her.

For years, I had collected songs I imagined learning to play someday. Paul Simon's "Me and Julio" and the entire Gillian Welch library. Because Kara's house was on my way home from work, I started spending one evening each week there. I arrived, stack of printed-out chords and lyrics clutched in my hand, and Kara and I spent those evenings teaching each other our favorite songs. I asked her one night where she had learned all the things she knew about playing the guitar, and she said, "At music circle."

She was referring to a weekly event at the learning center where a group of local musicians gathered to jam on traditional tunes, each one taking a turn choosing and leading a song. I had attended music circle a couple of times and had not found it to be a place to learn the kind of skills Kara had. "You Are My Sunshine" and "This Land Is My Land" were favorites at music circle, which did not account for her working knowledge of major 7ths or lead lines. I mentioned to my friend Alice one day that Kara had learned what she knew at music circle, and Alice stopped whatever she was doing to gawk at me. "Penny," she said, incredulous, "Kara is a classically trained musician. You don't know who you're dealing with."

One night, after making our way almost to the bottom of a bottle of wine, I noticed the curve of her neck where it turned into her shoulder. The skin there, exposed by her tank top, was finely contoured, and I fixated on the way her shoulder then curved downward and disappeared beneath the fabric. I stared at that spot—the edge of her shirt—where her bare skin was covered and found that I wanted to nudge the fabric aside. Just a little. After I drove home that night, I fell asleep thinking about that place on her shoulder and the warmth it created in my muscles and on my skin. I sank into that feeling instead of turning the hose on it. The things that would have stopped me were washed away by the contents of that nearly empty bottle, and I let myself think the unthinkable, unicorn-level-impossible things.

Kara and I never sat down to play music without a bottle between us—sometimes two. We sat by her woodstove in winter, outside on her deck in summer, and always that bottle was there like a tiny monument. I like to think that I was drinking normally back then—that I was taking my time through each glass, pausing before I refilled, not scheming to make sure I got my fair share or doing complex mathematical formulations to see if, somehow, we could squeeze a fifth or sixth glass out of the bottle. That all came later when my drinking became, by any definition, not normal.

Wine pulled out all the stops. This is pipe organ terminology. A pipe organ is a huge contraption, requiring multiple tractor trailer trucks to deliver it. You need a ladder and strong quadriceps to tune it and patience to play it. The stops mute the sound—there's one in each pipe. When the organist wants to play at full volume, they pull out all the stops. The organ bellows, filling all the air in the room with sound. It's a giant set of bagpipes requiring the musician's full body.

Before it destroys lives, alcohol removes fear, heightens emotions, makes dinners into occasions, gives us a reason to go to California (despite the earthquakes and wildfires), and helps us unwind after a hard day of writing or bricklaying or brain surgery. It's an equalizer. A friend. A reason, an excuse, a justification, a prophecy. It's a sure thing. It's a river we can set sail on in sexy crystal stemware. It's also responsible for a lot of people having a lot of sex. Some of it ill-advised. Some of it not possible any other way. All of it hard to remember the next morning. It washed me onto the shores of another woman's body—unfamiliar (yet entirely familiar) terrain—by distracting me. It kept the guards busy while the possibility of this love affair eased its way in. It reached into those chambers, those pipes of muscle and movement, and pulled out all the stops.

Kara admits now that she was guilty. She fed the beast. She sometimes waited until I wasn't looking, then topped off my glass in hopes that I might find myself too far gone to drive home. Even before we shared a bed, she was regularly tucking me under a blanket on the couch in her living room for the night, and she liked knowing that I was in her house.

Our relationship was becoming like a bronco waiting in the chute. A pinball waiting for the shooter rod. A water balloon being filled, filled, filled, and filled.

One night, we practiced music in her living room, getting ready for our first performance. We had been asked to play for thirty minutes as an opening act for my soon-to-be-ex-husband's band. (When I say "we had been asked" it means "we offered," and my soon-to-be-ex-husband was in no position to say "no.") The night of the performance was coming up fast, and we decided to practice standing up instead of in our usual places on the couch or floor.

I stood, sock feet on her faux-oriental rug, facing the picture window that had gone to black. Kara stood next to me looking much more natural behind her guitar than I felt behind mine. In my memory of that night, she is wearing that same black tank top, and her dark hair is down, though I think my memory defaults to that tank top whenever it can't remember.

We were a rocket on the launch pad. A lit match near a pile of cedar shavings.

We stood side by side, facing the window, and sang something. As always, I had to stay in my head for this, to find the chords, to remember my harmony line. Musicianship never came naturally to me. It was hard for me to get lost in it the way Kara could. She could close her eyes and disappear.

When we finished the song, Kara reached for the head of her guitar and started checking the tuning. She was forever checking her tuning. She nodded toward the window. "Do you see how cool you look?"

Years later, I would play with a tuner permanently clamped onto the head of my guitar, as I never developed the ear required to tune without that external technology. I could sort of tune the instrument to itself—so that the strings were at least tuned to notes the right number of steps from each other—but tuning to a true note just by listening remained out of reach. To tune a string to its neighbor involves plucking both strings and twisting the peg until the notes match. As the frequencies near each other, the interaction between the notes creates a fluttering feeling in the ear that lessens as the gap between them closes. It's called beating, and it's more like a sensation felt in the body cavities—the chest, the ear canal, the throat—than it is a sound. As the two notes become one, the anxious beating feeling diminishes, then vanishes. When the pitches match, they do so without drama, without discomfort, without any flailing in the heart.

I looked at the window. The night had turned it into a mirror, and it showed us standing there, guitars slung in front. We looked like musicians. Looked like rock stars, complete with an empty bottle on the table in the background.

Without taking my eyes off that captivating reflection, I strummed my guitar tentatively, just seeing what that looked like. The six notes in the G chord I likely played rang together, vibrated the air in complimentary frequencies, hit my ear like a warm breath. The wine on my brain let me step outside myself and look at that reflection as if it wasn't me, and I saw a musician standing there playing her guitar. Standing there, looking not half bad in my jeans and T-shirt, hair pulled back into a ponytail, I could almost imagine backstage credentials hanging around my neck.

Kara smiled at me. "You look incredibly cool." And then she looked at me, and some kind of pulsing, urgent energy rushed into the room like a vacuum seal somewhere in the house had been punctured. I looked at her green eyes but also the edge of her tank top and also the bump and curve of her soft wrist. And somehow I felt her gaze bore through my clothes.

We were a corked bottle ready to blow.

# Gay Parties

Again I went to Georgie's alone. By then I was escaping as often as I could, easing the door closed, latching it, walking down the steps and to my car. Driving off, usually into the dark. The silence of my marriage had become a loud thrumming.

Another potluck. Another ethnicity of cuisine that I can't remember. Kara and I were almost a band now. We had a repertoire and a regular practice schedule. Unlike our acoustic instruments, our bond felt electric—charged.

Food knits people together, especially when it's served with alcohol, which is a scientific fact. A 2017 study published in *Adaptive Human Behavior and Physiology* concluded that laughter, reminiscences, and alcohol are statistically significant factors in bringing people closer together. Perhaps more surprising are the study's findings that dancing, chocolate, and party games make no measurable difference at all.

Had that study been published seventy years earlier, it would have been hotly disputed by E. O. Harbin, the author of multiple books of get-to-know-you party games. His 1950 volume *Gay Parties for All Occasions* advocated for parties called Let's Have a Circus, Let's Go Bear Hunting, and the very dubious Plantation Party, for which Harbin describes five different games involving watermelon, a game in which guests pick cotton balls from the lawn, an activity in which the "Plantation Players" perform a skit of *Uncle Tom's Cabin*, and instructions for refreshments that read simply, "Serve watermelon." Apparently, in 1950, white supremacy served to bring some people closer together—a fact that hasn't changed at all. So let's assume that Harbin was not progressive enough to have had Kara and I in mind when he wrote, "Parties are most fun when they are gay parties."

Midway through the party, Kara went upstairs with a headache. She described it as "crushing" and went to lie down. She had come prepared to spend the night, to avoid the long, dark drive home.

I listened to her climb the steep staircase to the double bed under the sloping roof of Georgie's old farmhouse. I heard her ease down onto the bedspread. I listened hard enough that I swore I could hear her let out a breath of relief to be prone and in semi-darkness. My attention was a current in the river fork, divided and fast. From the party below, I could hear every breath, every shift she made on the mattress. My awareness curved like taffy, down the hallway, up the stairs, into the eaves of the house where she lay. I brought her water. Tylenol. Felt her forehead with the back of my wrist. I clucked and fussed.

Drunk, I chaired a loudly agreeable discussion about presidential politics. Kara teases me now, repeating my loud insistence that the United States had elected "two hundred years of penises to the White House." It was time for a woman to take charge. I was too drunk to drive home. Georgie let me stay the night.

"You can stay, but I'm out of beds," she said, businesslike. "You'll have to share with Kara."

That simple, tossed-off sentence, in my memory, moved my mind's eye like a movie camera through the house and up the back staircase to where Kara still lay under the weight of her headache. If it had been a movie, there would have been the screeching sound of someone ripping the needle off the record. The whole party would have stood still for a beat while those words sank in.

I managed to say, "That should be fine." But it was like the searing hot woodstove in the kitchen. I needed to remember not to touch it. I had to hold still while the room spun itself around my wine-soaked head.

Later, I lay next to her in that darkened, slanted space. I don't remember it as an event as much as a feeling, a sensation, like a toaster dropped in a bathtub. Or like a sound, like a cracking, rolling peal of thunder. Lying next to her sleeping form in the dark, I felt like I was in one of those dreams in which every step I take bounces me thirty feet into the air. Step, rise, and then the crazy lurch back to the ground, step and rise again.

I wonder what E. O. Harbin would have called this game of Don't Accidentally Touch Her. I played it for the six or so hours between lying down and opening my eyes to daylight. I played it, by the rules, even while I slept a sleep made heavy with alcohol.

She tells me now that she didn't sleep that night, as she was adhering to the rules of Let's Be Statues. She was terrified that she might move in her sleep and that her leg would brush mine or her fingers would graze my skin. She wanted that to happen but was paralyzed into wakefulness by the prospect.

This is not how it's supposed to work, and by "it" I mean falling in love and by "supposed to" I mean some process that I imagine is standard for whatever normal couples experience, and I don't even know what I mean by "normal." This attraction was not merely forbidden—it was impossible. It was grow-wings-and-fly, lick-your-own-elbow, open-a-unicorn-farm impossible. We both tried to fend it off, but it was like holding off an advancing fog bank with our hands. It rolled and misted past our best efforts.

The next morning, I sat at Georgie's kitchen table with my hands wrapped around a hot cup of coffee. I was up before Kara, talking with the other overnight guests. I loved this kind of hangover—groggy and with a slight headache but not nauseous. I loved the clarity these hangovers brought to my day. It's sort of like the way sunglasses help you see better even as they take away light. Hangovers reduced the daily information to a manageable size, and I often felt more relaxed in their grip.

I chatted with Melissa, who was working on her PhD in literature. I talked with Georgie, who was always doing something fascinating: going to Africa, starting a business, buying a hive of honeybees. Then I felt a hand on my shoulder, just briefly, as Kara passed behind me on her way to the coffee pot. I listened to Melissa talk about the students in her class and their thoughts on Dickens, but my swirling, hungover attentions were fixated on Kara while she filled a mug and took the empty chair next to mine.

I moved into every corner of my skin then, as if I had never explored those places in the tips of each finger or the creases behind knees. My skin almost had to expand to encompass this new self, this glowing, seeking self that wanted to be much taller than it was. This self wanted to watch everything from ceiling-height, a bird's view of the scene. My memory of that morning is from somewhere ten feet above the kitchen table where Kara sat next to me with her cup of coffee and Melissa talked about comp lit and it was an act of will to keep the fingers of my right hand curled around my coffee cup instead of putting them on Kara's knee.

Harbin (despite his casual racism) was right about one thing. This game of Let's Not Touch served, somehow, to bring us closer together, and gay parties are, in fact, more fun.

I had packed up to leave, finally, and loaded the few belongings I had with me into the back seat. I said goodbye and thank you and tried to drive away, only to find that my old, red Saab would not start.

I came back into the kitchen and reported this. Kara looked at me, full-on in the eyes, and said, "Let me drive you home."

# Harmony of the Spheres

Acousticians, the physicists of sound, will tell you that sound is formed by waves of moving air particles. A tuning fork, guitar string, or pair of vocal cords vibrates, making the air particles around it move, which make more air particles move. A displacement wave takes shape, spreads outward, becomes a tsunami shoving air ahead of it. A series of sound waves create areas of compressed and expanded air, regions of high and low pressure. Humans have built devices to detect these highs and lows. Humans are, at times, these very devices.

Kara and I had been practicing. We had a gig coming up and had spent that afternoon with guitars strapped across our bodies, running through our songs. We stood in the warm sun of her dining room, all polished oak and golden-colored fabrics and candles and stones. The light poured in, molten, through the giant windows that overlooked the deck that overlooked the field and forest that was the yard. The room felt ignited. Our voices pushed into each other's. Harmony lines came easily to her, but they were hard work for me. Sound waves that come close together make higher pitches, and higher pitches are higher notes. Some frequencies sound good when they overlap, and some don't: the difference is that between consonance and dissonance. Combined pitches that don't sound pleasant are dissonant, and those that resolve into something beautiful are consonant, harmonious. Consonance and dissonance can be used in music to create emotional effect. Knowing when to use one or the other is important to expression. This is as true in relationships as it is in music.

To teach me a harmony line, Kara would record herself singing it so I could practice it alone in the car on the drive back to my house. I spent many miles, during this time of our relationship, singing the same chorus over and again, trying to learn the counterintuitive rises and falls of the harmony line. Melody is seductive in its familiarity, and part of learning harmony is forgetting melody. Our relationship took on that characteristic of forgetting and re-learning, letting go and reclaiming.

Pythagoras, the Greek philosopher and mathematician whom we know for the triangle formula we all suffered through in high school geometry, theorized that the solar system is as predictable and patterned as all the right triangles in nature. Surely, he thought, the distances between the planets coincide with the distances between strings on an instrument or notes on a scale. The planets, he thought, hum in harmony with each other when they orbit.

It's a beautiful thing to imagine the sun as the tonic note, Mercury singing the major 2nd, Venus picking up the minor 3rd, and Earth anchoring down with the perfect 4th. The planets become like members of a celestial choir, tones doppplering as the spheres exchange knowing glances and smiles as they slide past one another, singing eternally in harmony. A universe so ordered that it's recreated in piano lessons, Suzuki books, symphony orchestra pits, around campfires, and all the way to the bottom trenches of the ocean, where we imagine glowing, yet-to-be-discovered creatures devouring each other in perfect whole and half steps: the whole of everything turning and singing out a perfect minor scale.

This idea, the Harmony of the Spheres, was held as truth for a long time, but as the Renaissance slowly crept behind the sun and came back around as the Enlightenment, the theory was slowly, reluctantly shredded by scrutiny from a list of Who's Who in physics, including da Vinci, Kepler, Newton, and Galileo. The distance between Ceres and Jupiter or that between Neptune and

Pluto does not match the space between the A and D strings on my cello, but to the last, all those giants of the field seemed to want it to, for they all shared a passion for music.

One day, while working out a harmony line in Kara's dining room, I said, "By the way, I'm interested in doing some grant writing on the side." I had started writing grants at my job and found the process of turning words into funding very satisfying.

"Really?" she said, looking away from the sheet music. "That's so interesting because I think we're looking for someone to write grants now and then for the learning center."

Kara introduced me to her boss, who spent the next several months teaching me the voice of the learning center and the simple future tense of grant writing. I wrote grant narratives during the evening when my kids were in bed and executive summaries early in the morning before leaving for work. *We will create change. We will engage community members with possibility. We will start our own high school. We will enhance wellness. We will build and plant community gardens and teach food preservation. We will create harmony. We will upend lives.* Months later, the learning center advertised for a development director, and I interviewed for the job.

In my five years in the job at the domestic violence agency in Machias, I had sat with women while they cried over the horror their lives had become. I had sat with women while child protective services took children from their arms because sometimes the helping systems fall for the lies of the abuser. I had exited a woman from the shelter for harboring a man in her room; I found them happily eating a pizza on her bed. I had taken a hotline call from a woman forced to call us by the police because her husband had, in her words, "lost it." I gently pressed her to tell me what that meant, and it meant that he had torn apart their kitchen with a hammer, but he would be back and she couldn't leave her home because who would feed her horses? I had taken a hotline call from an elderly woman forced to call by her doctor. She didn't want my help, but she talked to me because that seemed like the polite thing to do. She couldn't leave, despite the violence she endured, because where would she go? Before the day of the double homicide, I had already designated my thirty-minute evening commute as my daily crying time. There were nights I could barely see well enough to drive home.

I arrived at work that day, hair pulled back, wearing a casual pullover shirt and jeans, the uniform of the nonprofit social services administrator on a day with no external meetings. From my desk, I could not see the front office door, but we had hung bells on it to alert us to anyone coming or going. I was the first one in the office that morning, and the bells were not ringing. The staff was late.

One arrived with information about some sort of problem on the south end of town. The police had blocked off the road. There was an ambulance. Then another one. Information slowly leaked into the office over the next hour. It was a murder. No, a double murder. Children were on the scene. An officer was dead. A woman was dead. We finally got her name. One of her children had been wounded. It was her ex-boyfriend who did it. Of course.

The phones started exploding with calls, and TV cameras arrived so quickly that I had to make a statement with my messy hair and social worker jeans. We could neither confirm nor deny that we knew her, as was protocol, but the red-rimmed eyes of the staff and general devastation in the air made the question irrelevant.

Amid that horror my phone rang, and it was the director of the learning center calling to offer me a job. The other phone lines were flashing, and the bells on the front door were jingling incessantly as media and law enforcement and others came and went.

"I'm going to have to call you back," I said. "But I'll take it."

# Quantum Music

"Kara, I'm curious," I said to her late one night. "Are you a lesbian?" We sat, guitars across our laps, and had I known how to pray, I would have beseeched the heavens for a "No."

I had been working full-time at the learning center for a few months by then. Our small staff of five shared the cramped second floor of a timber-framed building, our desks shoe-horned tightly beneath sloping ceilings finished with blond pine boards. The space was only two rooms. I was in one, and Kara was in the other. Our desks were separated by a wall, and I had to walk past her any time I went to the photocopier or filled my coffee cup. From my desk, I could hear the clicking of her keyboard. I didn't understand why, but I knew I was going to the photocopier more than I needed to and was drinking more coffee than was healthy.

But if she was straight, like I was supposed to be, the possibility of there ever being an "us" would go away. If she was straight, I could stop hovering in the space between what I thought was the real me and this other me that I didn't yet recognize. If she was straight, I could go back to being one person.

Today, it's the acousticians and the quantum physicists who are learning to dance with each other. In this world in which it's accepted that Monday and Thursday share the same space rather than being distinct from each other, what do we make of a C note being different from a G#? Is there a theory of quantum music that gets us from Mars existing on a guitar to a guitar not really existing at all and an A minor chord bonking around in a dark box next to an A major? Can a theory encompassing all of that still be beautiful?

In 2021 physicist Katie McCormick wrote, "While a composer works within a framework of music theory to produce something beautiful and interesting, a physicist is interested only in finding the truth of how the world works, regardless of whether that truth is beautiful or not." She wasn't writing about the truth of women being underrepresented in the field of physics, though that fact is also unbeautiful. She was responding to someone else's seemingly preposterous idea: that musicians could provide insight into the study of quantum physics. After all, she lamented, "quantum" had become a buzzword for anything mystical or unusual, including "homeopathy, dishwasher detergents, and deodorant." (She was right: you can, as of this writing, purchase a pack of eighty-two Finish Powerball Quantum dishwashing gel tabs or select Sure Quantum antiperspirant for men from the personal care products section of many stores, and it's unlikely that either of those products meaningfully seeks the truth of the world.) So, when she first heard the phrase "quantum music," she would have outright rolled her eyes if the idea hadn't belonged to the well-respected, male physicist Klaus Molher, who proposed that musicians, with their intuition for frequencies and how they interact, could bring something to the study of vibrating quantum particles. She restrained her eye-rolling, but her eyes "narrowed in skepticism" all the same.

Her article goes on to chronicle the centuries-long love affair between physicists and musicology, opening with Pythagoras and ending with that spoilsport Vincenzo Galilei, who defied everyone and smashed a system of tuning that had bent over backward to accommodate the beauty of the Harmony of the Spheres theory.

McCormick was skeptical of the efforts of these men to warp truth out of loyalty to beauty. Nonetheless, she relented and studied something called Bose-Einstein condensate, which is "a cloud of atoms that have been cooled down to just above absolute zero." When they're that cold, they become one entity, and she played around with software that coaxed "very strange" music out of the lump of condensate. It was, she concluded, beautiful in its own way. It was, she concluded, not such a terrible idea to let our love of beauty lead the way to some kind of truth.

"Where we run into problems is when we rigidly prescribe our definition of beauty, not allowing it to grow and develop as our music and our knowledge of the Universe do." The problem is never the truth. The problem is when we don't trust ourselves to find it.

Her answer was, "Yes. I'm gay."

When practice was over and I drove the thirty minutes home, it was a trick to keep the car on the road through the dissonant waves of sobbing that seized my body, leaving me gulping for air in the troughs between them.

## Tonal Regions

On June 4 she said, "We have to have a conversation."

We sat in deck chairs made of canvas slung off metal frames, and I had a beer bottle wedged into a mesh cup holder hanging below the arm of my chair. I got right to work peeling the label from the exposed section of glass. I stayed on task throughout the conversation.

Her deck overlooked a two-acre field. In daylight we frequently saw deer and rabbits in that field, and its airspace was visited by bald eagles. That night the field was dark, lit only by fireflies and light spilling from the windows of the house. We had spent the evening practicing music, and then we put away our guitars and wandered out onto the deck to finish our beers. I sat in a chair with my back to the house. Kara sat in another chair to my left, her back also to the house. This allowed us to stare out into the darkness instead of at each other.

Eight years later, in 2016, a musicologist and a mathematician from Finland published the results of their collaborative quest to represent sound in three dimensions. Using a 3D printer and vector physics and a bunch of math I'll never understand, they created a tiny sculpture of the 4th movement in Mozart's Symphony No. 40. It looked, depending on one's angle or frames of reference, like a scrub brush, a roller coaster, or a creepy, bristly slug. Their writing posits that not only are the objects that result from this process beautiful in their own right, but they also offer interesting opportunities for analysis of the music they represent. For example, the slug-scrub-brush reveals that Mozart's Symphony No. 40 "mainly moves around in its basic tonal regions. However . . . the final movement's development section is among the most remote in classical symphonies." It means that most of the notes of the piece are longtime neighbors who see each other on the regular at the grocery store and on the sidewalk. Only in the final movement does the piece let in some radical newcomers from far away. No matter how familiar or unfamiliar the notes are with each other, though, the frequencies of vibration of strings or reeds can become forever frozen in the tangible world of plastic, and we can carry them in our pockets, rubbing them smooth with the pads of our fingers like worry stones.

When she said the words, "We need to have a conversation," a shaking erupted from someplace deep inside my body. I took steadying breaths to calm the vibrating sensation that emanated from the center of my chest, but it persisted.

I kept my fingers busy peeling shiny gold paper from the bottle, grateful for the darkness that separated us.

"We do," I agreed, somehow getting the words out. Then, softer, "We do." I rolled a piece of shredded beer bottle label into a tiny round shape between my thumb and finger and flicked it into the night.

There was a long pause. Fireflies, held aloft by invisible, membranous wings, blinked in and out of visibility. We both intently watched the darkness. Ahead, the tree line existed only as a dark shape yielding abruptly to stars.

"I want you to stop me if I start to say anything that sounds too far off." Her words felt pre-measured, as if she was serving them carefully onto a plate.

I could only nod in the darkness.

"I've been thinking about you a lot," she said. "And I need to admit that I'm feeling a certain level of attraction." She approached the topic like she was defusing a bomb.

I had practiced this conversation with Kara so many times in my head while driving the geography between our houses that I practically had scripted it. My line was, "If there was a way to put this conversation off, I would. But we really can't anymore." I paused, realizing that it had sounded better in my head. "I know what you're talking about." The shaking made it hard to breathe.

I don't know what else we said. I have lost the transcript of who said what and in what order. Many of the details from this time are lost to me. The months of questioning everything I was supposed to be had turned my brain into a snow globe and shaken it hard. I knew I wasn't supposed to be thinking about this friend—not that way, not naked. Not in the shower. Not while I was writing and cooking and falling asleep. Not that way.

That night on the deck, we said whatever words we said that made us understand this: we both felt it, and it was not going away on its own. At some point, the night's sharp chill prodded us to move inside to the couch, where we sat under a blanket. We faced each other, backs to the couch's arms, and our feet met in the middle.

"I think about you all the time," was all I could say by the end, so I said it over and over. "All the time." My fingers laced with hers, and I traced the outline of her wrist. The thrill of her fingertips against mine had quashed the shaking. I wanted to touch more of her, to see what it felt like to undo someone else's bra. "All the time." Like Symphony No. 40, the conversation fell into a series of tones that all stayed within sight of each other, closed like a gated community where no new words were granted entry.

We made solemn plans to go slow. We vowed that our friendship was the most important thing and committed to brave edicts about not letting boundaries fall too quickly. I was married. I had work to do.

Amid all that vowing and oath-making, all I wanted to do was take her upstairs to her bed, but instead, I kept tracing the form of our interlocked fingers with my other hand and saying, "Kara, I think about you all the time."

We agreed that I could not spend the night. We were too weak to be trustworthy. I found my car keys, picked up my guitar, and left her house. She has told me so many times since then what it felt like for her to watch me drive away that night that my memory has shifted to her perspective. I don't remember leaving or driving away, but rather I remember watching myself do these things from the kitchen window that is now ours. The tears I remember on my cheeks are really her tears on her own cheeks, as I watch my own headlights tear through the silent darkness of that night and watch my own taillights disappear into the trees.

When I got home, I crept upstairs and eased into bed next to my sleeping husband. I had to gently move aside the kids to make room for myself, first Abby and then the baby. The familiar dark of our home had barely parted to welcome me back in. The mantle clock that was a wedding gift from his parents ticked and tocked audibly from the bookcase. The kids had stirred but stayed asleep—their dreams untroubled by what was about to unfold in this household. I did not sleep. I lay there, replaying the conversation in my head, remembering the softness of her fingertips. My chest resumed its vibrating and pounded its way through the night.

I look back now and wonder what a sculpture of that moment would look like. If someone were to sculpt the profound silence of the nighttime, the baby's soft breath on my shoulder, the whirring white noise machine, and my pounding, thrilled, terrified heart and represent it in a lump of polymer, would it be as large as the moment itself? Would it be shaped like a ready-to-erupt volcano, hell-bent on taking out the peaceful-seeming homestead on its slope? Or like the A-bomb dropped from the *Enola Gay* onto Hiroshima? Or would it be small and smooth like a beach stone or a marble I could cup in my hand and protect in ways I would later want to protect these children?

# Rose Garden

It was newsletter week at the learning center: a period of days that came twice each year. Other work almost stopped while the whole staff, and some volunteers, spent all day collating, stapling, and folding newsletters, affixing labels to them, and sorting them into bulk mail bins. Kara and I spent Thursday, June 5, the day after the conversation, moving through the rooms, around the newsletter pages, staplers, and chatty conversations like it was our job not to make eye contact with each other. I don't remember how we got through it without imploding, and the details of the next day's hours are equally lost to me, except this one. I was not at work on Friday, June 6, because I worked a flex schedule that allowed me to have Fridays at home with my kids. I left the house that day only long enough to stop by the learning center to deliver an item to Kara—a CD with the Dave Matthews Band song "Say Goodbye" burned on it—along with a postcard. The front of the card was an old-fashioned, hand-colored photo of a man and a woman in passionate midkiss, with text that read, "He was not as fascinating as he had once appeared." On the back, I wrote, "Ok, so this is slightly naughty of me—crossing a boundary here and naming it. As I drove away from your house, this song randomly came on. Interesting." It was a bold move. The song is about two friends who decide to be lovers just for one night—just to see what it's like.

I handed her the CD and left, saying, "I'll see you later."

That night Kara's other band was playing at a café in Eastport called the Rose Garden, and John and I had secured a babysitter so we could go. It had been open for a couple of years in a town where many businesses didn't make it past their first February.

The owners, Linda and Al, both wore dreadlocks down to their waists and served up salads, veggie burgers, and cheese steaks from a kitchen somewhere behind the bar. The tables were wooden, painted white, and the seats were molded plastic lawn chairs. The place was also an antique shop, so much of the décor was for sale. You could stop for lunch, have a beer, and purchase yourself a brass lamp or a stuffed jackalope in one stop.

Kara shared the stage with her bandmates, Jim and John V., and three jade trees with white Christmas lights strung through their stubby leaves. I sat, with my husband, at a two-top to Kara's right. We were positioned so that I could lean my elbows on the table and stare directly at the band, and my husband had to turn in his lawn chair to see.

My friends Katie and Alex sat at the next table with their daughter and her friend. They had driven almost an hour one way to be there that night, not so much to hear the music but to support me. Alex's story had a plot similar to the narrative that was now unfolding in my life: married to a man, in love with a woman. She had eventually left that man and had been with Katie for over a year. I had called her the day after the conversation. "You won't believe what's happening."

"Actually, I bet I will."

They sat and occasionally looked at me, nodding reassurance.

Kara can tell the story now of being onstage that night and being so grateful for the presence of our friends. She had someone to look at other than me, seated with my husband. She had listened to the Dave Matthews song on the way home from work that day, and I now know she listened to it on repeat all the way to Eastport. I had closed my note to her with, "You are a rock star tonight, and I will hold our secret like a jewel in my pocket. Sing it to me." She watched me share a meal with him. Watched us engage sporadically in conversation with our heads close together so we could hear over the music. She worked hard to stay on her game, hit all the right notes, strike the harmonies. I worked hard not to let anything seem different there at my table as I made small talk with the man I was married to. Kara's eyes locked with mine for seconds at a time. Information and reassurance passed between us in those moments, and we held those gazes for as long as was comfortable. Then one of us would break away, to tend to a conversation or study a chord, letting the moment go by. I bought myself a glass of wine at the bar and paid for an additional one to be delivered to her onstage.

At some point in the evening, my husband went home to relieve the babysitter. We had agreed that I would stay out longer, listen to my good friend Kara's band, and get a ride home from her. Car keys in hand, he gave Kara a friendly wave as he strode to the door. I leaned back into my lawn chair, beer bottle in my hand, and stared openly. I let myself take in her long hair, the guitar pressing against her hip, and the way she had closed her eyes as she sang.

Katie and Alex eventually left too. We hugged. Katie squeezed my arm. "This will be fine." They waved at Kara as they walked out.

The audience continued to dwindle until it was just me. Kara, Jim, and John V. decided to pack it up. I helped roll up cords, put mics in their cases, and zipped mic stands into a long bag. Kara and I moved through these familiar tasks without looking directly at each other, trying to rely on body memory alone. Jim brought his truck around, and we all loaded the gear into the back. Then Jim went home, and John V. stayed to have a couple of beers. He perched on a bar stool to order one up, and Kara and I left the room together through the cavernous adjacent warehouse full of antiques. In the back of the room, behind all the tables displaying old dishes, animals made of pinecones, and porcelain dolls, was the entrance to another, smaller room with two pool tables. We sat on a used futon with a price tag on it and talked. But only for a few minutes before she lifted my hand, took my finger into her mouth, and let her tongue play across its surface.

I did the same with her fingers, and the sensation drove us onto our feet and into the dark privacy of the pool room. She leaned her back against the pool table and reached out for my belt buckle. She pulled me against her, and we kissed. It was a deep kiss. It was my first kiss in the Hallmark way that says a first kiss is supposed to change everything. What I remember more than the kiss, though, is the feeling of her fingers grasping my belt buckle, the insistence in that tug. My body warmed up, ready to be wanted. Kara, emboldened, lifted my shirt, lowered my bra, and kissed one of my breasts. I think I stopped breathing.

We stopped, motionless, when we heard John V.'s voice calling for us in the other room. We straightened our clothes and our hair and emerged from the dark pool room. "Yes, we're ready. Let's go."

John V. was a stonemason and a fiddle player. He frequently showed up at gigs with masonry dust still coating his boots and clinging to the hairs on his sturdy arms and legs. I hold pictures in my mind of John at summer gigs in shorts, a T-shirt, and heavy workman's boots with his gray hair curling around the edges of his baseball cap. The dust followed him everywhere. He worked hard building chimneys and walls for people across the county, putting in long days hauling and lifting rocks and fitting them into place. John V. brought this same workman's ethic to his drinking and engaged in it with dedication and skill. Our driver for the evening, he outdrank us both.

We moved to another bar across the street called the Happy Crab. It was a standard-issue, coastal Maine summer restaurant: surf and turf, lobster, chowders, and a dippy name trying to capitalize on the locale. We bought drinks and took them to seats near the pool table.

Kara wrapped her fingers up with mine under the safety of the table, with our stonemason friend across from us and a group of men playing pool behind us. I don't know what made us think we were invisible, given that there was no tablecloth to hide what we were doing. The solemn boundaries we had sworn to were just two nights behind us. They rolled out with the night's fog.

After a couple more drinks, we piled into the cab of John V.'s truck for the ride home. Kara sat in the middle, and I was against the door. Not one of us was sober enough to realize that not one of us was sober. John V. played the harmonica, steering the truck with his elbows.

On our side of the cab, under the safety of a coat and the privacy of night, we groped and fondled each other. Her hand was in my shirt. My hand was on her inner thigh. The truck's headlights swept across the foggy causeway.

In the life of almost every recovering alcoholic, there are vague memories like this one. It should have been clear to all of us that nothing about this was acceptable. That we got away with it without arrest or tragedy does nothing to remove the truth of our selfishness and stupidity. If I could do it over again, there are so many things I would do differently. That dangerous drive home is only one of them.

We arrived at my house, where my husband and children were sleeping upstairs. John V. came in for another drink and stayed to play music outside on the deck. It was past midnight. I remember lying down on the cedar planking of the deck that my husband and I had gotten married on with all our friends and families looking on. My cheek against the scratchy wood grain, I listened to John V. play the fiddle. Kara sat with her back against the house, guitar across her lap. Dutifully trying to follow the tune, she watched John V. closely, tried to read his cues, tried to anticipate where his fingers would land next.

My fingers gripped the neck of my guitar, but I did not play.

John V. went home. His truck hadn't even reached the end of my driveway before Kara and I were pushing each other's clothing aside. We were like magnets, held apart then finally allowed to snap together.

When I reached into the front of her pants and felt the flat, triangular patch of hair there, I said, "You're just like me."

She recounts that moment now with amusement, wondering if I expected something else. But it was a shock to have my hand between a woman's legs, to reach away from myself only to find something so familiar.

I was unskilled and clumsy, and we were both trying to be quiet, aware that my husband and kids were asleep in the room directly above us. They were all in one bed, underneath the wedding quilt.

On a futon in my living room, we were naked under a blanket, feeling our way across each other's bodies. It felt like making love to a mirror image of myself, with all the parts in the same places, all her responses so like my own, her sharp intakes of breath familiar. Eventually, exhaustion set in, and we slowed our explorations, then stopped. We lay there, not saying anything. Then I heard a sharp sound I couldn't identify. It was chirping that grew louder. I asked, "What is that?"

She shifted, getting ready to rise from the tangle we had become. "Those are birds."

"Why are birds singing in the middle of the night?" I watched her reach for her shirt.

She looked at her watch. "Guess again."

# The Encyclopedia of Good Mothers

In the language of weird, abstract math, quantities are either scalar or vector. Knowing the difference involves determining the qualities of the quantities. Do they have magnitude? Do they have direction? Do they have both?

Vector quantities, such as force and displacement, have both size and direction. People who understand vectors can predict how far a cannonball will travel and how much damage it will do. They can calculate a safe flight speed and path through cross-winds. They can design roller coasters.

Scalar quantities, like temperature and speed, have a magnitude but lack direction. We use scalar qualities to talk about how hot it is outside or calculate the area of our living room before we shop for carpeting. Most people understand scalar quantities better than vectors. We relate better to anything that, like most of us, lacks direction.

My straight marriage was like this: it was enormous for the way it involved my children, our conjoined extended families, and our identities in the world, but it wandered aimlessly, drunkenly in no direction at all.

Kara's departure early that morning was a vector. Using all the hugeness of what had just happened as a kind of rocket fuel, she launched herself in one clear direction: out the front door and on the road home.

She was barely gone before I had to leave.

We had risen in the fading dark to the tentative sounds of birdsong, and I held her before she left, told her that I loved her. She kissed me, then was gone. I watched her headlights flash down my driveway, then taillights, then darkness. I watched the place where my driveway meets the paved road, the place where her taillights had disappeared behind the neighbors' trees, still feeling her hands on my body, on the back of my neck, between my legs, in the small of my bare back. The sky, across the road and over the water, had just begun to lighten. I had not seen four a.m. since college. In two hours, my kids would want breakfast.

I climbed upstairs and slid silently into bed beside my sleeping husband. In a few hours, we were leaving for a weekend at his parents' house. In a few hours, I would have to pretend that we were still married.

John's parents lived in Bristol, Maine, in the summer and Naples, Florida, in the winter. It was early June, and they had just returned north. They hadn't seen us, or their grandchildren, since the fall and were anxious for a visit. That morning I got back out of bed and stepped back into my real life as if it were a pair of slippers. I fed the baby his bananas and milk, fed his sister a bowl of Cheerios, and packed their things for the trip. I collected coloring books, crayons, and stuffed animals and arranged them in the back seat of the car for the ride. While packing Goldfish crackers, cups of apple sauce, and juice, I thought about her—her mouth on my neck, fingers in my hair, the way she had touched me, brought me to climax instantly. Bleary-eyed and dehydrated, I talked with John about the day ahead—where we would stop for lunch, what we should remember to bring. I wondered if he could see that I was having an affair. Was it on my face like a tattoo?

On our way out of town, we stopped at the learning center so I could drop something off. It was Saturday morning, and the community gardening group was there, preparing plots for the season. Kara was there, overseeing their efforts. We had talked about this moment before getting out of bed just hours earlier.

"I'll have to stop by with John on our way out of town," I had said to her, my naked body pressed against hers under the blanket.

"I know." Her fingers played with a piece of my hair.

"I'll be with him, but you know how that is." The "that" was my disastrous marriage.

"I know." She sighed. "But it's hard anyway, to see you with him."

John and I parked the car. I went into the building and put my laptop away for the weekend. I was looking for her, but she was outside, in the garden, avoiding me—avoiding me with John. When I came outside, while John was waiting for me in the car, Kara came around the building. She wore shorts and a T-shirt, a baseball cap and sunglasses. Her dark hair was tucked up under her cap, and there was freshly tilled soil on her feet. Our eyes couldn't exactly meet because of the sunglasses, but some electricity held my feet to that spot on the ground. There wasn't time and this wasn't the place to say anything other than goodbye; I hugged her quickly, the way someone might hug their coworker, and I whispered, "I'll be thinking about you." Then I was gone, rushing off like a hurricane, like a displacement wave, shoving everything in my path ahead of me and letting it accumulate on the blade of my plow.

We met Andrea at the Railway Village in Boothbay Harbor. She brought her son, Isaac, who was almost two years older than Abby. John, his mother, all three kids, Andrea, and I wandered around the grounds, fed the goats twenty-five-cent handfuls of grain cranked from dispensers into the kids' hands, and leaned over to look at the incredible details of the electric model train that took up an entire room. Tiny conductors held lanterns as trains ripped past tiny stations and fields of tiny livestock. Tiny signal lights that really worked directed the comings and goings of little black engines pulling coal and passenger cars. The clarities offered by one-way train tracks, stop lights, and station signage offered a welcome structure to my otherwise unclear world. I could place the growing wave of displacement on a track, aim it toward the goat pen or even farther toward the coastline, and let it vector away from me.

Andrea was one of my oldest friends. She lived near the town where John had grown up and where his parents still spent the summer, and we had planned this excursion weeks earlier. As our group rode on the real train on a track that circled the entire park, when the others were crowded around windows, looking out at the real-sized livestock and real-sized signal lights, I leaned in close to her ear and said loudly enough to be heard over the clacketing train wheels, "I'm officially having an affair."

She pivoted in her seat. "What?"

It was one of those spring days on the coast of Maine that feel like a revelation after the long winter has staggered away like a drunk finally leaving the bar. There's a phase in early spring when the snow is gone, daffodils, chives, and rhubarb have forced their heads out of the dirt, and the swarms of biting bugs have not yet hatched; it's a time of year that reminds us why we live in Maine despite the frost heaves, conservative politics, and lack of a major airport. Spring in Maine is a long, sensual process in which nature unrolls herself on her own schedule. First the woodcock, then the peeping frogs and the first flowers, then the wild plum trees and forsythia, and a green haze so delicate it almost hurts drapes itself over the landscape.

With that spring stretching its limbs around and over us—so full of hope as to make us feel like we could burst—Andrea and I slid away from the group as often as we could so I could fill her in on the ways I was imploding my life and ruining my family. I spoke the details softly so the others couldn't hear.

Inside the mock train station: "It's with a woman."

Outside the model train room: "It started with music."

In the back aisle of the gift store: "Yes, we're having sex. Just before I drove down here."

In the room with six hundred pairs of salt and pepper shakers on display: "I might be in love with her."

In the parking lot, while the kids bought ice-cream cones: "I don't know what to do."

She listened, wide-eyed. Andrea and I had enough in common to be considered the same person, or so it seemed at times. Her ex-boyfriend, Isaac's father, was John's best friend, and that relationship had turned disastrous, much as mine was. We loved the same books, loved to write. We both made our living as grant writers and could spend hours geeking out together over the intricacies of requests for proposals and how to write a compelling ask. Years later, we would attend the same MFA program. But as far as I knew she had never slept with a woman. She was rapt, caught in both shock and curiosity.

After we had seen all there was to see, including the collection of antique internal and external combustion engines, the display of carriages from the 1800s, and the blacksmithing and barrel-making tools, we all gathered on the porch of the gift store. The kids licked up the rest of their ice cream, and Abby and Isaac started playing with some fuzzy white caterpillars crawling on the bushes next to the store. Members of our group, now standing close together, entered the kind of chatting indicating that a visit is almost done. *What are you doing with the rest of your day? Is your garden in yet?*

John's mother asked Andrea how things were with Josh, which was a loaded question given his state of absentia from the life of his son, who had been born prematurely, was left with some ongoing health challenges, and was being raised without any substantial support from Josh. Andrea said whatever kind, socially acceptable thing she said, and at some point, later in the day (as she did on so many other days), John's mother commented that *Josh is a good father*, an opinion she had formed by seeing him, on occasion, not utterly failing at keeping Isaac alive. Such is the standard we hold for good fathering. I don't know, because I never asked, if my mother-in-law had ever commented that *Andrea is a good mother*, but I believe I can assume she didn't. To be notably good at mothering required things neither Andrea nor I would ever do, like not having careers we loved and remaining devoted to the fathers of our children. If there were deal-breakers, actions that guaranteed exclusion from the Encyclopedia of Good Mothers, having an affair with anyone—especially another woman—was surely one of those actions.

Abby and Isaac let the caterpillars crawl up their bare arms and across their shirts, laughing at the tickling feeling. Isaac's ash-blond hair shone like metal under the sun, and Abby's brown curls bounced as she laughed and squirmed. I noticed a faint redness starting to appear on the undersides of her arms, then I lifted her shirt. Her chest was covered with a rash that seemed to raise even as I looked at it, and it was advancing like a line of uncontrolled fire down her arms.

"The caterpillars," urged Andrea. "Get the caterpillars off them."

Abby started to cry. We fled from the train museum and drove straight to the drug store for Benadryl. The prickly hairs from the caterpillars had lodged in her sensitive skin. In the back seat, while John drove, I held my crying daughter to my chest, tried to soothe her, to make her understand that this was no big deal—just her skin's reaction to these bugs that we all thought were fun.

"I didn't know that could happen," I said to Abby, though I said it loudly enough for everyone in the car to hear. I thought back to all the caterpillars I had touched in my life, how I had let them inch their way along the back of my hand, from finger to finger, their little feet like suction cups on my skin. I didn't know any of this could happen.

# Please Don't Notice Me

I had spent years developing relationships with John's sister and brother, their spouses, his parents, all the nieces and nephews. I had shopped for Christmas presents, made travel arrangements, tried to participate. The first time we went to New Jersey to visit his sister for Christmas, I baked and brought three dozen homemade biscotti to share. I planned, shopped for, and made a salmon dinner for everyone one night. I smothered the salmon in sautéed leeks and sundried tomatoes, olive oil, and salt. I whipped sweet potatoes into creamy perfection and served it all in John's sister's perfectly appointed dining room with shiny round chargers under all the plates and matching sets of shining cutleries all lined up on cloth napkins. I had paid dues for this membership. That weekend, as we all gathered and shared stories and drinks, I started untying the knots that held me to these people.

Back at home, Kara was living out the weekend knowing that I was among his family. She gardened and read books and tried to keep her feet under her.

John and I stayed in a back bedroom, with our kids in sleeping bags on the floor around us. I chose the side of the bed closest to the door. Crawling into bed each night with him, after an evening of drinking and talking with his family, I felt like the mattress might be filled with crushed glass or sharp nails. To move, to shift my body under the blankets, felt like it could hurt.

The bedroom was tiny. The double bed took up most of the floor, leaving just enough room for the kids to unroll their sleeping bags next to it. John's mother loved frilly, Victorian-looking décor, and the dresser at the foot of the bed and both side tables had lace table doilies draped across their surfaces; making the bed included replacing a small mountain of lacy, hand-painted decorative pillows on top of the quilt. The lamp on my bedside table was small and delicate, and I felt misplaced in that room among those fragile things. I felt like my body was a huge, destructive force, like my fingers shouldn't be trusted to work the scrolled metal of the lamp switch. I might break whatever I touched. I might step on the kids in the night. I might knock something over just moving through space. Something frilly and fine might get tangled in my awkwardness.

John and I put our suitcases on the floor of the closet and tried to keep our things orderly during the visit. John inherited his sense of order and fineness from his mother, and keeping his clothing and belongings neatly stacked and sorted while traveling was never a problem for him. He saw it as sort of an obligation—especially in his parents' house—to fold his clothes, place them neatly inside the suitcase, and to set his shoes next to each other someplace out of the way. I was always happy to shove my clothes into the suitcase, let the dirty ones accumulate someplace nearby, and leave my other things (jewelry, paperbacks, notebooks, pens) strewn across dressers, tables, the floor. But not that weekend. That weekend, I played along and kept my clothes (even the ones I had worn already) in my suitcase, kept the lid of the suitcase closed, and even did a load of laundry in the amazingly clean and ordered laundry room. I tried to keep all my flaws hidden. I feared that my infidelity might show through them.

One night that weekend, John and I went to the movies together. We had parked the car and were walking toward the doors of the theater, and his hands were in his pockets. He cocked his elbow toward me, jauntily inviting me to slip my arm through his. I took the invitation and put my hand on his arm. We walked forward that way, entwined, until we didn't.

# Earth, Wind, and Fire

Twenty-five hundred years ago, Aristotle wrote in *Historia ani-malium*, "Lines are not written into the human hand without reason." He also wrote, "The inner surface of the hand is the palm, which is fleshy and divided by lines; in long-lived persons by one or two lines which go straight across, in short-lived by two which do not go straight across." Some theories conclude that palmistry, also called chiromancy, has origins in ancient India and then spread throughout the East.

*Llewellyn's Complete Book of Divination* says, "Palm reading is mentioned at least four times in the Bible. Probably the most famous of these can be found in Job 37:7, 'He sealeth up the hand of every man, that all men may know his work.'" I'm certainly not a scholar of the Bible, but to me that reads like it could just as easily be referring to the miracle of unique fingerprints or maybe the importance of work gloves, but humans have a long history of seeking weird tools to understand the future and other stuff that makes no sense.

Kara was given a palm reading as a gift, and she then gifted one to me. Each reading was a two-part process. These four meetings were scheduled in a way that wove them between the significant events of this time. Kara's first one was the day between the conversation and the Rose Garden, and the second was nine days later, when we had already slept together and a tidal wave of problems was in the act of crashing down on our heads. My first reading was two weeks after Kara's second one, and my second one was five days after that. The specific dates and the timeline are less important than the fingerprints this time left on our bodies, hearts, and lives. These readings were recorded on cassette tapes, and listening to them now brings us back to how our voices sounded, how we presented to the world, and the simultaneous fear and joy we felt for simply being seen.

First, the palmist analyzed the shape of our palms. Were they square? Oblong? And what did that reveal about us? Hand shapes are deemed to belong to the elements: air, earth, water, and fire. Even though astrological signs are linked to these same elements, a person's sun sign (the one we look for when we check our horoscopes) need not match the element of their palm shape. I'm a Libra (air sign), but my palm is either earth or fire. Kara is a Pisces (water sign), but her palm is all about the steadfastness of earth. Do these discrepancies strip meaning from these interpretations or deepen them?

In the second sessions, Louise the palmist offered interpretations of the lines on our hands and our fingerprints.

A print of Kara's hands revealed strong earth tendencies but with a lot of air showing up, and a scar she had on her finger was there to tell her something about either her relationship to money or her self-esteem rather than being a reminder to be more careful with sharp objects. Something on her left palm led Louise to say, "There's some emotional turbulence going on in the area of intimate connections. I don't know if you have a partner right now. Are you with someone?"

Kara's reply, after a beat of silence and breathing, was, "What an interesting question. Maybe I could be vague on that right now."

Later, Louise said, "What's showing up is that you're not clear what road to take."

There are, according to Louise, four schools of life: wisdom, peace, service, and love. Kara's fingerprints put her in the school of wisdom. "It's also called the school of denial," Louise said. "Just about everyone who is in it doesn't believe they are."

After describing that the school of wisdom is focused on being more vulnerable, less risk averse, and taking plunges rather than sitting on the fence, Louise said with no small amount of excitement, "Are you ready to hear what your life purpose is?"

On the tape, Kara waits silently.

"You are supposed to be a creative artist in the spotlight. You are supposed to express your individuality. Coming from the school of wisdom means you need to be ready to take the opportunity to display your gifts. Be careful about procrastinating."

Louise went on, "Your life lesson is what will challenge you. Yours is called feeling not enough. It's a belief that, no matter what you do, you might not be enough."

When it was my turn, we learned that my hand and fingerprints revealed the potential for conflict between my earth and fire tendencies and that I could either suffer through it or learn to milk it. She also identified me as someone who processes out loud, is comfortable with authority but not too much, and should not join the military.

"Have you ever been called mercurial?"

"No."

"What about moody?"

"Yeah, maybe."

She asked, "Do you think you are flirtatious?"

I paused, then said, "That question comes at an interesting time, and I'm going with yes."

Interestingly, she said, "There's a writer's fork in your head line on your right hand. Nonfiction is what's showing up. It's a nonfiction writer's fork."

My fingerprints placed me in the school of service, and my life purpose was a heady three parts. I was to be successful, have a public impact, and focus on healing arts. "People like this can be authors," she noted.

She concluded by saying, "You are someone with a lot of passion who loves excitement and is learning to use their power."

When Louise said to both of us, "You need to be understood," she was not speaking specifically about Kara and me. She was speaking about the conditions of our lives, our shared existences.

Palmistry, like other occult arts, gives us much to be skeptical about. Like numerology and astrology, it exists outside the boundaries of science. Or does it? Astronomy and astrology both began when humans started to wonder about the stars and planets, and back in the good old days of planetary harmonics, physicists and mathematicians were drawn to numerology because its chances of explaining the unexplainable seemed as good (or as poor) as other available theories. Palmistry, unlike some of its pseudoscientific cousins, turns the lens away from the stars and onto the human body. It's more like phrenology and physiognomy than it is like astrology and numerology for the way it positions the body as the point of entry into the mysterious workings of the universe and the longstanding quest to understand the human condition. It's not faith-based, but it also totally is because it draws on our faith that there's some tangible principle at work. Even better than something we can touch, our fingerprints are themselves the surfaces with which we touch anything and anyone.

# Counterfactuals

ME: I don't want to be some big disaster in your life.

HER: What about the flip side? Some fantastic miracle?

ME: I guess I'm more experienced with disasters than miracles.

HER: I'm not breathing very well at this moment.

If you visit the wikiHow page for "How to Not Get Caught Cheating," there's a handy list of steps you can take to hide your infidelity from your partner. You can set up a fake email account, partially clear your browser history (fully emptying it will only look suspicious), avoid putting telltale charges on your credit card, and purchase separate birth control supplies. The page also offers a crash course in Gaslighting 101 by explaining how to take your partner's suspicions seriously while simultaneously dismissing them. "Don't laugh in a mean-spirited way, and don't make fun of your partner for having their suspicions. Simply act surprised or bewildered by the suspicions, as though it never would have occurred to you that you were acting in a questionable way."

Fortunately (or not), this resource was not available to Kara and me during the weeks that our affair lived underground. We protected our secret by trying to maintain the appearance that nothing had changed. We failed in these efforts at work: our coworkers sensed the difference, though nobody said anything.

We communicated slyly (we thought) in writing. Facebook had recently become a thing we all used, and instant messenger became the motel room we met in as often as we could, which was all day, every day.

ME: I want you to get this—you could put down the music tomorrow—it wouldn't change this.

HER: Well, that's a lie, but thank you.

ME: It's not a lie.

HER: I might need a cold shower.

ME: I might need an inhaler.

Around us, our work lives ticked past. The photocopier, next to her desk, filled the office with the ka-chunking sound of promotional materials and grants. I came out of my office to put in more colored paper, and she lifted her gaze from her fingers to meet my eyes, her response to my response broken off mid-sentence. The restraint felt physical—like a harness around my chest—and I was swinging like a pendulum between my desk and the photocopier. In between, we kept messaging, kept trying to find our way.

Though it is standard now for employers to have policies that discourage and restrict workplace romance, it's estimated that this is precisely how one in three marriages begin. I look around now at couples I see tucked into booths at restaurants, holding hands on sidewalks, pushing strollers bursting with babies and toddlers, or ignoring each other in favor of scrolling on their phones, and I wonder—of every three couples: Which of them began over Post-it Notes, flip-chart paper, printer jams, or corporate retreats? Which started by bumming a cigarette on a loading dock? Who among the throngs in an airport met their true love in a stock room, over a cash register, or while setting up tables and steam trays at an event? Did anyone now sitting in the waiting room of the couples counselor learn their future spouse's name by reading it off the nametag pinned to her apron? And among those that did, how many of them had someone else at home? Someone who was picking up Legos, dropping off the mail, stuck in traffic, or dreamily making vacation plans for a minute while stirring a cup of coffee? Who among all those couples we see in all those places are the ones who smashed their homes apart? And of those, how many had partners who cared?

ME: Are you ok?
HER: I am.
ME: Promise?
HER: Yes.
ME: Have you laughed today?
HER: I feel a little sad.
ME: Me too. We want more than we can have right now and that's hard. I love you and I know you're still there and still with me and still in this.
HER: I'm still here and in this.

This experience of operating covertly, with our hardest conversations taking place with us in separate rooms, has left us sensitive to each other's energies like tuning forks. I learned to decode her feelings through punctuation and lower-case letters. I can tell now just by how she moves through the kitchen in the morning what kind of day we're likely to have. She would say that I fool myself into believing this, but I first learned to read her face when her back was to me because I had to. This, too, is a counterfactual, for it's not possible for me to look at her back or hear her footsteps or pick up a clear tone of voice in a text message and instantly be able to see her face, but there is no unified physics of life yet. The Italian physicist Chiara Marletto writes, "Declaring something impossible leads to more things being possible."

I could see her through the wall, hear her in a font.

ME: Staring at the screen now.
HER: I'm thinking about last night.
ME: Specifically . . .
HER: Tracing your fingers, how hard it was to not dive in or at least wade in a little farther.

We tried to work, tried to create programs, write grants, answer phone calls, go to staff meetings, but whenever we could we took ourselves to our computer screens. It feels weirdly geeky to remember our romance like this: colored printer paper, the font of the newsletter, the staplers and tape dispensers on our desks, the paper cutter I walked past to get to her desk, looking at each other across the table in staff meetings.

When I was a kid, sometimes my mom took me to work with her, and I remember feeling drawn to the little closet of office supplies on the second floor of the converted farmhouse that served as offices for Maine Indian Education. She worked for a state agency that oversaw educational opportunities and scholarships for members of the Passamaquoddy Tribe, upon whose land we live. At the time, I didn't recognize her work as being minor redress for colonialism or genocide. I only knew that, at her office, they had shelves with rows of bottles of Liquid Paper used to paint over typos, and it came in pink, blue, yellow, and white to match the delicious reams of paper that were delivered by the case. They had boxes of paper clips and gleaming, pristine staples. There were tape dispensers, new scissors, boxes of pens stocked like ammunition. There were reams of paper that came pre-punched with holes for three-ring binders, and there were boxes of the binders themselves. And if you wanted just one hole or many more holes or holes in alternate places, there were hole punches. You could also use them to create a blizzard of tiny, perfect paper circles that even the vacuum cleaner couldn't easily pluck from the short, scratchy fiber of the office carpeting. On everyone's desk, there was an IBM Selectric typewriter, the machine on which I later took typing class in high school and to this day still covet. They turned on with a smooth toggle switch and hummed into readiness. By swapping out one walnut-sized ball for another, you could change the font from courier to script, from bold to italic. I regarded this technology as a visitor from the future: something magical and space aged. I wonder now what my first-grade self would have thought if confronted with the idea of a typewriter that could instantly send words through a wall, could complicate and deepen the beautiful mess I was making, could simultaneously explode and implode my identity, could propel me into the world of being othered.

HER: Have you considered the added hardships of (possibly) having a relationship with another woman? That's one thing I worry about for you.

ME: Oddly, that's sort of the thing I'm the least worried about. Which may indicate a certain level of cluelessness.

HER: Telling your parents . . . experiencing judgments. Having friends or family ditch you.

ME: It's hard to talk about this . . . I don't carry a high level of concern around it. And I recognize that, as such, I may come across as having a lack of understanding for things you have gone through. I probably am clueless.

Let me be clear. I did not choose to upend my identity and my life and enter the world of the other, but I also did make it a choice. Marletto also wrote about the need for counterfactuals, "statements about which transformations are possible and which are impossible in a physical system." That I both did and did not have a choice in this transformation does not seem like it can be true, and yet it is. This distinguishes me from my neighbors in this world of the other in ways that rise to the level of life or death. It's dangerous to be othered in America.

# Why We Got Divorced

As I try to understand how so many things can be true at the same time, I take a long strip of paper and write, "This is one version of the story" on one side of it. I flip it over and write, "This is the truth" on the other side. After creating one twist in the strip, I staple the ends together, making a Mobius strip. A story with two sides now just has one.

John and I sat in the kitchen, and the kids were in bed. At least, I was sitting. He may have been leaning his back against the counter or the sink. I was sitting on a barstool at the narrow, small table that served as an island in the expanse of our kitchen floor. We both had mugs of hot tea in our hands.

We were not arguing but had fought so many times before this moment. We had hurled words, crashed them against each other like sabers, stalked away from arguments, and then come back together, resolving to do better. We had taken these fights to the brink of decision, time and time again, but slunk away when we stared into the gaping chasm of what a separation really meant for our kids. Holidays apart, summer vacations split in two, someone always missing out on something, dividing up the Legos, animals, and Candyland.

We did not argue about me being gay. We did not fight about Kara. We were not in conflict because I harbored a secret. We argued, and needed to divorce, because we should not have married in the first place. We married because I wanted to have kids, but having kids doesn't make a bad relationship into a good one. We divorced because I wanted a different life. I wanted a different culture. I wanted off the island of the American working mother who, after working full-time, was expected to grocery shop, make dinner, do the emotional labor of managing all familial relationships, pump breastmilk, puree and freeze organic vegetables for baby food, co-sleep (aka, not sleep), and do it all again the next day. Those gender norms—and they are deeply internalized and prefer not to be acknowledged—did far more damage to this marriage than my eventual transition.

One night John and I fought with such high emotion that he picked up a guitar stand and flung it at the wall. It penetrated the sheetrock and stuck there like a javelin. I don't know what we fought about that night, but it was something far more pedestrian than my sexuality.

Two weeks after I started sleeping with Kara, I knew it was time to tell John. I said, "We need to do something about us." I was ready. I had a solution.

He did not ask what I meant. This topic was always in the room. "I know."

"I think we can split up but do it differently than most people." I was calm. Practical. Like I was discussing a strategy for car shopping or repairing the furnace. I had thought about this. "We can put the kids first and create something that works for them." I went on to describe some utopian scenario in which we built an addition onto our house—an apartment for one of us to live in. I fed these fantasies, in myself, for a couple of years after the split, still believing that we could do this better than most people. In the end, we really didn't. He agreed, though. "I think we need to do that. All of it. We can't do this anymore."

A marriage that took years to build ended in the time it takes to drink one cup of tea.

It took me three days to bring up the rest. In my memory, we are in the same positions: me at the table with my feet resting on the low rung of the barstool, and John leaning against the sink.

I said, "There's one more thing."

He waited.

I said, "Kara and I . . . ," and it's here that my memory falters. What verb did I use to describe what Kara and I were doing? Dating? Sleeping together? Having an affair? Whatever I said, he understood.

In fact, what he said was, "I know."

There was a beat of silence.

He added, "I think Kara's great. And I think you deserve it."

This conversation took even less time than the first one.

It's amazing to me now how easily we let it all go, how easily we slid into this life apart, into a life in which our kids have to do all the traveling between our homes. Like the way it's easy to slip your arm out of your husband's when you reach the ticket counter and it's time to dig money out of your purse. You just let go.

# Coming Out

Coming out is like using a road map. It's awkward and full of creases, and once you get the thing unfolded, you'll never get it back in the glove compartment. Instead, you'll stuff it in the pocket of the door, where it will ride next to your left elbow as the miles roll under your radials. Eventually, you will need to consult the map again. It will unfold more easily each time because its creases will be more defined and your hands will be better at finding the edges, but it will never look like it did the day you bought it. Sometimes you might fold it so only the panel you need is visible, and then you'll re-fold it once you drive far enough east or south to warrant exposing more. It will exist in this half-folded, half-open state until you need it entirely stowed. Younger generations, when you pull out your map, will laugh at you and wonder why you're still using a paper map anyway.

Kara and I told our boss first, though it seems he had known for weeks. We had not been as subtle as we thought, flirting back and forth in the small office space we shared with three coworkers. Our workspaces were defined not by walls but by the placement of our desks, file cabinets, and sloping wood ceilings. These intimate quarters made anything private—phone calls, one-on-one conversations—impossible. The truth of Kara and me had snuck up on the two of us, but evidently it had been more obvious to those we worked with. I convinced myself, and Kara, too, that I could take in every inch of her with my eyes during staff meetings, imagine what her skin might feel like under my fingertips, and nobody would know. But I had not convinced anyone else.

Coming out is not an act. It is a process composed of a thousand acts, a thousand conversations. It happens every day, every moment, every time someone asks, "So what does your husband do for work?" A gay friend described to me recently that even after twenty years, she still gets what she referred to as a butterfly in her chest when faced with questions about her husband. She quells the butterfly—a beautiful moth—and gently corrects, never knowing what the consequence might be. Coming out never stops.

When we told our boss, we weren't yet practiced in the art of coming out. The information was too new even to us for it to roll easily out of our mouths. Now, the words "partner" and even "wife" have worked their way into the vocabulary of our relationship—the cells that make up our interactions, however uneasy, with the world. But when we told our boss, we were still protective of the news, still shielding it from light, keeping the sun off its skin. We cradled it, kept it swaddled. But we told our boss because we felt he needed to know. The three of us, plus his wife, were about to take a weekend trip together, to a concert on the other side of the state. Kara and I had bought tickets and put the invitation out to our coworkers months earlier, before we even knew ourselves, and our boss and his wife took us up on it. We all had tickets. We all had plans. Kara and I wanted the option of a hand on a knee, perhaps a long embrace, an arm draped across shoulders. We wanted to be a couple that weekend. And so we told our boss.

Kara dove in. "So, Penny and I have fallen in love." She reached over and put her hand on my knee. "And we wanted you to know that so we wouldn't have to hide this weekend."

I was not prepared for her forwardness. I had imagined that we would wade into the water more slowly. But there we were, immersed. I felt it running down my back, dripping off my eyelashes.

Days later, I got in the car and drove the half hour to my parents' house—the one I grew up in—on a day when I knew my mother would be there alone. The house sat on twenty acres of deep, Maine forest. As a kid, I had spent summer days, almost feral, running through these woods. Clumps of cedar rose out of the wettest part of the property, forming walls for clubhouses or castles. Trails, cut mostly by my father for skiing, transected the property, and though they were uneven and marked by roots and rocks, I used to ram my pink bicycle with the banana seat along their length, bouncing and occasionally getting thrown off. Right next to where I parked my car that day were the remains of a small vegetable garden I had planted and tended as a kid. Held up by four stubby railroad ties, the plot was maybe four by five feet. There are photos of my twelve-year-old self standing proudly on the edge of that garden, looking right at the camera, holding a hoe. I wore a blue velveteen shirt, and my hair hung long and unkempt. Whoever took the picture asked me to pretend to use the hoe, so there's another photo of me diligently whacking at an imaginary weed growing between the tomatoes and the beans.

The house was simple—a square two-story with cedar shingles that my mother had dipped by hand, one at a time, into gallons of stain the color of rust. I remember them arranged for drying, balanced on their thin edges, leaning against each other, across the basement floor. They looked like a maze. As a child, I had helped her with this, and in my memory my father is outside, on a scaffolding, and we can hear the steady beat of his hammer driving the stubby shingling nails through the thin cedar, adhering row after row to the side of the house. And we are surrounded by the cool cement of the basement, dipping shingles one at a time and then leaning them artfully against the accumulating sculpture.

As I shut my car off, next to my old garden plot, my eyes swept across the flat surface of those shingles. Stain had been recently reapplied, this time with a brush, and the side of the house fairly glowed in the sun that day—the color of a pumpkin lit from within. I took a breath, got out of the car, and walked toward the back door.

I let myself through the gate made of driftwood onto the deck my father had built and entered the kitchen through the back door. The dogs, three of them, swarmed around my legs, all tongues and tails. My mother sat reading the newspaper in the sunroom. She was expecting me. Though she sat reading the paper and appeared relaxed, I knew better. She closed the paper as I entered the room. She sat in a wooden chair with curved arms that my parents had owned my entire life. It was pulled up to a table made from a giant wooden spool, the kind that electrical cables come on. Its surface was pocked with cracks and insets for bolts but had been varnished to a high gloss by my father decades ago. I had grown up with it serving as our kitchen table and had spilled many glasses of milk by accidentally setting them in one of the divots. It also had holes that went clear through to the round inside of the spool. Many items—spoons, saltshakers, small toys—had been dropped into that void and then fished out through the opening provided by one missing slat in the barrel-like body of the table. I had grown up wishing for a normal kitchen table, like my friends had, one that wasn't made of recycled anything. One that had four legs and a flat top. One that didn't say "hippies."

I sat down in a chair opposite her.

She took off her glasses and waited.

"I've met someone," I began, immediately forgetting whatever version of this announcement I had practiced in the car.

She nodded, and I could see her brace her jaw against some imagined pressure. The news of my divorce was only a month old. My mother was a kind person—frequently baffled by the cruelty or stupidity of others. She was also a political person, and she taught me what I know not about choosing battles so much as winning them. If you're right, stand up and say so.

"It's Kara," I said, feeling like I was dropping a bomb on my life. "I've fallen in love with Kara."

Coming out is a road trip. There are miles and miles of highway, indistinguishable from each other when you think back on them. Telephone poles, guard rails, dotted yellow lines firing past, the occasional stop to pee, another Diet Coke. But you remember the high moments—the national parks you might visit, the amazing vegan restaurant you found tucked behind the gas station, the stranger who helped you change your tire late at night. You also remember the low moments—the moment you heard the tire start to flap, the day your money ran out, or the moment when the huge cement truck cut in front of you, nearly wiping you out, and you had to slam on the brakes. Those moments leave you breathless and shaking, trying not to think about what might have just happened if not for those lucky few inches of space. You might curse the person behind the wheel in the cement truck while your heart claws its way from your throat back down to your chest cavity.

Kara told her parents in a phone call. I wasn't there, but I imagine her using the same flat-voiced directness that she summoned when we told our boss. "I've met someone. It's a woman. We are in love." Her dad asked why she had never mentioned being gay before, and she said, "Because it never mattered before."

We told our brothers. We told our friends. Coworkers. The reactions were as mixed as the ages, backgrounds, and life stories of the people we told. Someone said, "I think that's great." Someone else said, "I don't believe in that." Someone else said, "I don't care." Yet another someone said, "I'm going to out you to other people because your story belongs to me now." Another person said, "I'm worried about what this means for your kids." Another person said, "Yes, I already know."

Coming out is a choice to stop passing for straight. It's a choice to join the resistance, to admit that you're more than just a sympathizer. When you come out, you exit the building with your fingers laced against the back of your head, your elbows out— you have surrendered to the other side. Your uniform is stripped down, your colors are showing. Coming out is a decision to hand over your privileges, to turn in your membership card to the Not Other Club, but white, cis people like me can sneak back into the clubhouse with an expired set of credentials when we need to. When the restaurant server asks, "Two checks?" I can make the choice not to shatter their assumption that Kara and I are just friends. When we walk down a sidewalk together holding hands, we can let go midstride and become invisible again. If I were one of the Passamaquoddy people who live in this community alongside white people like me, there would have been no credentialed thirty-nine years of passing. My hair, black with shades of eggplant, along with the melodic lilt of my voice that you hear over on the reservation, would have made it impossible to luxuriate in the relative safety of the closet. My Passamaquoddy neighbors and I shop at the same convenience store, deposit our checks at the same bank, and get our oil changed at the same service station. The truth is that, mostly, I am grateful I can make my difference invisible when I need to. I am the minority tucked inside the majority. I can pass. This makes me complicit.

At my birthday party, there was a keg of rich, brown beer. There was a deep, dark chocolate cake with an acre of candles on its summit. There was a bonfire. There were friends with instruments playing music. There were kids running through the house. There was a rousing version of "Happy Birthday to You" sung in the kitchen as Kara swung around with the cake— seemingly aflame—held in her hands. The warm glow lit her face from below.

A carload of my friends—all straight, all moms—arrived together, helped themselves to red plastic cups of beer, and gathered around the bonfire. One of them elbowed me and said, "So where is she?"

Another one, standing across the fire, said, "Yeah, we want to meet her."

They all had the same, gawking quality on their faces. As we talked, their eyes only alighted on my face sporadically. They scanned the crowd, taking in the details of Kara's home, as if they were looking for clues.

Coming out is a sporting event: it attracts spectators.

There's a running joke, started on *The Ellen DeGeneres Show*, that if a gay person recruits enough straight people to become gay, they get a toaster. (Straight people don't seem to know this joke. At least I didn't, until someone pointed my browser toward the toaster-themed merchandise available on the internet.) This joke worked its way into our banter, and I regularly mentioned to Kara that I, as the recruitee, was also deserving of a small appliance, especially since she already had a toaster.

The morning after the birthday party, we were in pajamas, drinking coffee. She disappeared into a back room for a moment and came out carrying a large gift wrapped in newspaper. She set it on the floor in front of me. "Happy birthday, baby."

I kissed her before I peeled away the taped-on strips of wrapping. It was an electric rice cooker. I sat amid the crumpled paper and the box with Kara sitting next to me, and we laughed and kissed. The party was still on our skin, and the sun was lighting up the inside of the house. The hardwood floors glowed like they were lit from underneath. We laughed until we stopped, and then we cried. I had to go. I had to leave her there, to clean up the rest of the beer cups and the plates with cake and liquid blobs of ice cream.

It was my son's fourth birthday, and there was a party for him being staged at my ex-husband's house. Kara could not go with me. This day was about my son. My father, my mother, my son's father—all would be there, and it was just too complicated, too soon, for us to be that kind of out. I sat on the glowing wooden floor of her house, with the rice cooker in my lap, my forehead against hers, palm cupping the back of her neck, fingers laced up in her hair, and we cried together.

Coming out requires combat boots. It requires showing up with a bayonet in your teeth and your hand on the pin of a grenade. You have to be ready to break some things, take some people out. It leaves scars. But over time, it fades into the background of your story, the way that war shapes nations but eventually becomes just some full-color pages in a textbook. The next generation doesn't even care that it happened. We barely remember, day to day, how the simple act of saying who we were caused roads to wash out, villages to be swept away. We have let go of the life vests, now able to stay afloat on our own.

Ultimately, we told acquaintances. I told my aunt and cousins. Over the course of years, telling people evolved into the act of existing near people and telling them by using words like "partner" or "wife." Over the course of more years, we told the family garage where we got our cars fixed and the landlord and the school bus driver and the farmer who sold us squash and beets in the fall. We learned to approach interactions like we were minesweepers scanning for danger. If there wasn't any, we relaxed into the kind of normalcy that straight people enjoy without realizing it.

# Pink Capos at the Lobster Party

Georgie had a few couples over for lobster. She wanted us all to get to know her new boyfriend, Bill, though in this small town we already knew him. By now, Kara and I were performing together regularly enough that people knew us by those shows. Together, we were a folk duet called the Pink Capos. A capo is a specialized clamp that, when put in place on the neck of a guitar, changes the key. My first capo was silver and black, but when I saw that Kara had a pink one, I had to have one that matched. Our band name sprung from my adulation. Georgie had requested that the Pink Capos bring guitars to her lobster party.

The weeks prior had been spent in the murky arduousness of revealing ourselves and our relationship. My parents. My husband. Our boss. Each conversation had felt like the explosion of a depth charge, the shock waves shaking the water to the very center of the earth. The lobster party, where everyone either already knew or didn't care, felt like slipping upward through the surface tension, coming ashore, and toweling off in the sun.

I sat in the kitchen with Kara, Georgie, and an assortment of party guests. We played a Patty Griffin song, "Useless Desires." My chair was pushed back from the kitchen table enough to get my guitar into my lap, and I was uncharacteristically finding the harmony line exactly right. The science of sound includes the math of harmony. When a tuning fork is struck, the frequency of the sound waves determines what note we hear. When two tuning forks are struck at the same time, whether those notes are dissonant or pleasant is determined by how the two frequencies interact with each other. The waves of one note will not completely match the wave frequency of another, but to be in harmony the two frequencies must match sometimes while otherwise giving each other wide berth. If the two are too close, the sound takes on an uncomfortable, beater noise: what we hear when one instrument is out of tune with the other. It's that feeling when only one car window is down, and the air starts to flutter and pound. For notes to harmonize, they must be close but not too close, which is exactly how relationships work.

When I breathed in the scene, it felt like the air made its way into every part of my body, bringing light to all the dark places. We were together. We looked together. This was the love that everyone talks about. It's the love that's on Hallmark cards and in movies. It's the love that inspires artists to compose symphonies, paint murals, write odes that smart comp lit students have to analyze a century later. It's the love that people go goofy over, the kind that makes big pink hearts literally jump out of the chests of cartoon characters. It's a fireworks display so close that you can feel the booming and cracking right in the center of your chest, and it's also the quietest spring night when you can just start to hear the first peepers singing in the pond. It's getting lost on a road trip, finding the most amazing little art gallery in some wonderful village, and just buying a house right there and never leaving. The love that makes you stupid, makes you write clichés that feel brilliant at the time. I sat at the kitchen table feeling full of myself, puffed up, like maybe we were the first two people in the world to have found love like that, like we knew something that nobody else knew.

Love is as grand as the poets say, but it pales in comparison to relief. I felt relieved of some kind of death sentence, like the governor's office had called when I was already strapped into the chair and someone's hand was on the lever. Sitting there in the kitchen, with my hand now on Kara's knee, fingering the creases in her jeans while she talked with someone, the rest of my life waited out there for me. My husband was at home in the house I owned with him, my parents were still staggering around under the news of all this, and there was the matter of my children to figure out, but it felt like a turbulent flight was ending and we were approaching the safety of the runway. I listened to Kara laugh. She lifted her hand, without looking at me, and put it on mine.

# Provincetown II

The next time I went to Provincetown, eleven years later, the sandwich place had been replaced by a creperie, and John had been replaced by Kara.

Kara and I keep a photograph on our refrigerator of me at the creperie. It was taken so late in the fall that it's almost winter, and the deck is wrapped in translucent plastic walls to protect customers from the coastal wind and damp. My back is to the street, and I am wearing dark, reflective sunglasses and gazing directly at the camera, directly at Kara. I am smiling the relaxed, lazy smile of someone made fluid by hours of early morning lovemaking in an antique oak bed on the second floor of a bed and breakfast right in Provincetown proper. Behind me, through the plastic wall, the buildings across the street, the hand-holding passersby, and the aluminum ocean beyond are blasted out in white October light. In this picture, I'm not interested in the cerebral experience of marveling at gay couples being openly in love, for I am too busy experiencing it myself. On my face, there is no trace of the memory that I ever sat on that same deck sharing a sandwich with a man.

It was Women's Week. All season in Provincetown, it's this-or-that week—festivals designed to appeal to tourists looking for a reason to make the drive to the fingertips of the Cape. Women's Week consisted of all-female revues, female musicians, and female stand-up comics. The irony of a celebration of one gender in the town where gender matters less than anywhere else was lost on us, as was most of the festival. Kara and I had been together for all of four months. That's four months of coming out in a small town, four months of divorcing my husband, four months of parenting my two young kids through the rubble that their childhood became, and four months of trying to understand that sexuality is a continuum rather than a place. Who we love is a journey, not a fixed set of coordinates. We had lived those four months under the kind of pressure that causes fermentation, and Provincetown felt like the cork had finally been pulled and our love was allowed to sparkle and bubble as it slid down the sides.

We joined the very same parade John and I had watched years earlier. Up and down Main Street, we browsed for T-shirts and earrings, stopping to kiss at every opportunity: against the brick façade of an art gallery, under the brilliant orange canopy of a shade tree, in line to buy tickets to a drag king show, and again while we shared a chocolate ice-cream cone on a park bench. Bicycle bells rang out as residents navigated the throngs, trying not to run over any strolling tourists. On our way back to the bed and breakfast, I kissed her on a street corner as two men walked by. One said tauntingly, "Oooh, girls kissing." We didn't even look his way, for his smile was evident in the lilt of his voice. I pulled her closer. Kissed her harder. The sound of feet shuffling on the sidewalk moved past us. There was a tree arching above us, its leaves in transition from green to yellow to dust. Beyond that, the Cape Cod sky was a late afternoon silver, and it felt so close we could almost touch it.

On our first night, we slid into a booth at a busy restaurant, ordered drinks, and celebrated our decision to take this trip. We clinked our wine glasses together, toasting each other, new love, old love, freedom to love whom we wanted, and being on vacation, eating in a nice restaurant. Surrounded by red vinyl bench seats and mirrors on the walls, we toasted the excitement of being in a busy tourist town with art galleries, boutiques, shops selling wooden and glass bangles, sparkly scarves, packets of note cards wrapped in cellophane with impossibly crisp corners, tank tops with pictures of beach cottages across the chest, and wall calendars with photographs ranging from the scenic to the near-pornographic. One store sold clothing on the first floor and nothing but dildos and other sex toys on the second. Pastel-colored missiles in dusty boxes spread across what seemed like acres of tabletops. We browsed through these items with all the seriousness of people shopping for a new food processor or a coffee maker, comparing the various settings and features. At a newsstand I bought a rainbow bumper sticker in the shape of a cowboy boot. Before we drove home, I peeled the slick backing off and adhered it to the window of my old, black Saab. A couple years later, the frame of that old car rusted through, and I sold it to the junkyard. I like to imagine the sticker still visible after coming out of the crusher—a small bright spot in a vast jungle of twisted, rusted metal. Provincetown is that small, bright spot.

# The Largest Canyon on Earth

Four months after Kara and I started sleeping together, I described the situation to my new therapist.

"I still live in my house with my husband and our kids. I have the bedroom, and he's moved into his art studio. We think it's easier on the kids this way." That word—"easier"—felt so relative. There wasn't much that was easy about moving around my kitchen early in the morning, walking past my husband while he stood at the sink, while I made coffee to bring upstairs to the girlfriend who waited for me in my bed. She and I could hear him down there, doing the dishes or listening to the news, while we curled our legs around each other's and started our day with steaming mugs of coffee.

"And what about your girlfriend?" She glanced at her notes. "Kara? Does she come over?"

I squeezed the sides of my water bottle, popping the plastic inward, then back out again. "Yes. Kara comes over a lot and stays with me in the bedroom."

"The bedroom that you used to sleep in with your husband," she clarified.

"When you say it, it sounds weirder than it is," I said. "It's actually all okay." I thought of that bed and the two of us in it. When she was next to me, when the quilt I used to sleep under with my husband was slipping down and exposing her shoulder and part of her bare back, when she was reaching for my hand and bringing it to her lips, it didn't seem weird at all. Not even with my husband sleeping elsewhere in the house and the kids sleeping across the hall and the fire cracking and snapping in the woodstove in the room below.

"Do the three of you hang out together? Make dinner?"

I wanted this therapist to understand that we were doing our best. "Yes, we do. We eat dinner together, watch TV. Talk. Kara and John get along really well, actually." I thought about the three of us in the living room. My girlfriend watching episodes of *Battlestar Galactica* with my husband while I dozed with my head in her lap.

My new therapist was a tall, butch lesbian with little round glasses. She was leaning forward in her chair—in the listening position. She was quiet for a few beats, then asked slowly, "How does Kara fare in this? Is it weird for her to be hanging out with your husband?"

I assumed that it wasn't any more or less weird for her than anything about the rest of the situation. Nobody meant for this to happen. "I'm sure it is. I mean, the whole thing is weird. We know it is." I became very interested in the edges of the label on my water bottle and started picking at the paper intensely.

My therapist let a silence settle on the both of us like snow. She held that space with her presence and breathing until I stopped picking at the label and looked up, meeting her eyes for the first time since I started telling the story.

"Listen," she said, "you need to move out of there. Immediately."

Nothing about that rang true to me. Worse, it rang of laziness, a lack of imagination, like caving into societal expectations of people who divorced. I resisted this well-intentioned advice much the way I would resist well-intentioned, and ultimately accurate, advice from many therapists yet to come. In the future, I would get advice to quit jobs, to participate in weirdo treatments involving eye movement or holding buzzing electronic orbs in my hands to address the PTSD that lingered from the car accident, and to quit drinking. I resisted it all, convinced that I could find a different—better—way if I tried hard enough, worked hard enough, strained and struggled and innovated hard enough.

I was afraid of moving out. I was afraid of imposing a life of being split between two households on my two-year-old son and my four-year-old daughter. It's an oversimplification to say that I was staying for the kids, but it's also the truth. I didn't want to give them up every Wednesday and Thursday night and alternating weekends and holidays.

John and I both imagined we were beyond the need for separate living quarters. We were so over all that, so much more evolved than other divorcing couples. Our marriage had been over for so long, we didn't even need separate spaces.

The house we had purchased and lived in—the one with the rocking chairs and lilac tree—wasn't small, but it wasn't big in any of the right ways for all of us to live there. Two bedrooms. One bathroom. And so we shopped. We looked at two-apartment structures, large, sprawling old farmhouses with bedrooms and half baths down narrow hallways and up spiny staircases where people could live for years without running into each other. We looked at a property with two houses: a slightly dilapidated main house with a completely dilapidated guest house in its yard. The main house was remarkable only for the large, dirty cistern in the basement, which looked like either a giant toilet bowl or a bathtub-shaped portal to Dante's Inferno. I was uncertain that I could even sleep in a building containing such a thing and knew I would never be able to go into the basement as long as it was there. The guest house was remarkable only for the way that its sloping floors made us both wonder why it was still standing and why the realtor was showing it to us.

We moved on to a plan in which we would share the house we already owned together and invited a carpenter friend over for coffee. He sketched drawings of a two-story, one-bedroom addition off the kitchen. We paced the terrain, measuring distances and imagining an extension to the foundation—something that could support all these ideas. The addition would add a bedroom, a living room, a bathroom. It would involve new stairs.

It was a new concept, and not just architecturally. I remember a late-night Googling session during this time in which I went looking for examples of divorcing couples who lived together. I found a feature story about a couple in Canada who were doing just that: they weren't together anymore, but for the sake of the children and the sake of their financial health, they shared a house. Thrilled, I scrolled through the comments on the article, in which random internet people lambasted the couple for their selfishness and bad parenting.

There was work to do before we could move ahead with even this incremental plan. First, we needed to create democratic sleeping quarters: one of us needed to move out of the queen-sized bed in our bedroom. Before it was determined who that would be, it was the kids who needed to move out. Somehow it had evolved that all four of us shared that bed. This arrangement had not arisen out of any deeply held beliefs in the tenets of attachment parenting. It had arisen out of our need for sleep. It's easier to nurse a baby who's next to you than it is to cross the hall. And once a baby is used to sleeping next to you, it's just easier to keep them there, and so we had made this mistake, twice, of never teaching our kids to sleep in their own beds. The four of us had been crowded in there together for years, arms and legs tangled, knees and elbows bumping and pushing into backs, heads sharing pillows.

Neither of us was willing to be the one to move out of that arrangement, leaving the other parent snugly in bed with the kids. And yet, since we could no longer sleep in the same bed, it all needed to change. Now I see that cleaving for what it was: the first step of a separation that would unfold for years. The family unit, split like an atom, dispersing throughout the upstairs, then through the whole house, then across two houses—a mushroom cloud silently unfolding after we turned two red keys.

We decided that we would take turns sleeping on the floor of the kids' shared bedroom until they were comfortable and sleeping soundly through the night. Kara was traveling for two weeks, on an annual trip with her friend from college. They were camping in the Southwest, around the Grand Canyon. Her absence meant that I would be in this house every night, making it the perfect time to do this imperfect thing.

I went first because I am their mother and owed it to them. I made a bed for myself on the floor out of camping gear and tried to make it feel like some grand adventure. "It's like we're camping," I said. Owen was only two, and his sister was four. I wanted them to feel like this was something fun, something new, something that big kids did.

The first night, I tucked Abby into her big-girl bed. She had bought into the adventure. From under her yellow, sunflower-patterned comforter, she peeked down at my sleeping bag and pillow and giggled.

But when I plunked Owen in his crib, he stood in his footed jammies, leaning against the railing, his small arms reaching out for me, and screamed. I lay down on my camping pad, just about two feet away from his crib. "Owen, baby, it's okay," I cooed, trying to convince us both. "I'm right here, sweetie. Just lie down." He shifted from one jammied foot to the other, reaching out for me with both arms, his face red. He screamed for me. His cries were dramatic and insistent. The crib railing pressed into his ribs, and he reached harder and harder in my direction, his chubby little legs working hard to stay standing.

In those cries, I heard every mistake I was making, those I had already made, and all the mistakes sure to come. I heard him come up against our future of holidays spent away from one parent or the other, of split summer vacations, of watching someone move out, of living in a small town with a gay parent. I curled into a ball and whispered to him through my own crying while Abby drifted off to sleep amid the noise. I don't know how she did it. In my mind, that sound was the loudest in the history of sound—it was horror-movie loud. It was all-pervasive, taking-all-the-air-out-of-the-house loud.

Amid this horror, Kara called from somewhere near the rim of the fourth-largest canyon on Earth where the cell service is terrible, and when I answered I was crying so hard that it scared her. I choked out enough words, so she knew what was happening, but she had no time to reassure me before the call dropped. I hurled the phone into my bedding and surrendered to my son's frantic screaming. I don't know what happened next, but I have to believe we both slept at some point because it's over a decade later and he's a teenager who sleeps late on the weekends. To my ears, though, the screaming sound didn't stop for years. It didn't stop until I took all the advice from all the therapists. It stopped after I quit the bad job. It stopped after I participated in EMDR treatment. It stopped after I quit drinking. Until all that happened, Owen's screaming sat in my brain, a counterfactual to all that was happy and good and right about my transition out of that house and into our new life.

Ultimately, John and I were entirely average in our post-divorce living arrangements. There was no house we could buy and no money to build onto the house we had. There was no path forward into this utopia of parenting, though I would berate myself for many years for this failure to deliver us all onto the shores of this perfection.

On the day I moved out of the house, I borrowed a truck and loaded it with half the dishes, half the books, all my clothes, and half the toys until the shock absorbers sagged. There was no room for the kids on this first trip to Kara's house, which was now to become mine as well. The plan was for John to deliver the kids to my new home that same afternoon. We theorized that involving him in the move would reduce the permanent damage to the children that I was certain I was causing.

But Abby didn't understand the plan, though I had explained it using words she knew. "Mommy and you and Owen are going to have a new house. It's going to be fun." She understood, but when she saw me climbing into the driver's seat of a truck packed with my belongings, she screamed. She screamed, "Don't leave me!" as I started to get behind the wheel. I reassured her. Cheerful as I explained the plan, I told her not to cry. "This is going to be fun!" I started to drive away, but the sound of her begging rang in my brain, and I stopped the truck midway down the driveway. All ten fingers wrapped hard around the steering wheel, I cried gasping sobs—I froze there for what felt like hours—then I stuck to the plan. I drove away.

I have made mistakes. That was one of them.

# Breakdown

As program director, part of Kara's job was to run the Maine Expedition, a two-week wilderness camp for teens, every summer. The group spent the first week backpacking in Maine's northern mountain range and the second week canoeing the Penobscot River, which winds its way through the North Woods, passing near the base of Mount Katahdin.

As development director, it was assuredly not my job to deliver canoes to the Expedition when the group spent a night in Millinocket, but I did it for two summers anyway because we were a small staff, it wasn't anyone else's job either, and it was an excuse to see Kara once during the trip and to spend a night together in her tent, though I brought and set up my own tent to avoid creating any questions for the group of teenagers she traveled with.

The first summer, I traveled with our IT director, Kevin, but the second summer I went alone. I drove the learning center's ten-passenger van up 95, met the group at their campsite, spent the night, then helped them get gear, boats, and themselves to the put-in spot, and I helped Kara deliver the other van to the take-out. This involved a lot of driving on dirt roads but yielded a few precious hours together.

Before she had left for her trip to the Grand Canyon the summer before, I had given her a gift: a small, blank notebook with a panda, made by layers of cut paper, on the cover. The paper was fibrous and rough, containing such huge pieces of matter that to write on some pages involved navigating the words around what seemed to be entire sticks embedded in the paper. An explanatory note was included from the book's manufacturer: "Believe it or not, what you are looking at is a totally unique gift made from odorless and naturally recycled panda poo poo." From her tent in Grand Canyon National Park, Kara wrote,

I feel the small stones that poke into the tent floor, and I feel the chill in the air. At the same time, I imagine I feel the brush of your hand on my back, your tongue on my fingers, your breath in my ear, your lips on mine. My imagination is strong, Penny. It has been a long time since I've felt this mix of attraction, friendship, desire, equality, confidence (my own), want . . . all rolled into one and focused on someone who is mirroring most of the same stuff back. What an adventure we are stepping into here—an immense, challenging, rewarding, magical adventure.

The night before she left for the river portion of the second Maine Expedition, I took the book from her and wrote in it so she could read it on the river:

When I drive away tomorrow, I will cry. But the tears will stop. And I will remember that I still have you. I will remember that you and I still have our arms around each other, even when we are apart. I will take a breath, move forward from that strong place of love and faith; and I will count the hours until I hear the bus pull into the parking lot on Friday. Take my heart with you. Keep it (and you) safe and dry.

That morning, Kara, the other trip leader, and I worked through the vehicular logistics. Kara and I dropped the group at the Roll Dam put-in and circled back and dropped one van at the take-out at the ranger station at the southern end of Chesuncook Lake. The next leg was to drive Kara back to Roll Dam to reunite with the group, so they could begin the trip. It all took hours of driving up and down a long section of the Golden Road, a wide stretch of dirt traveled only by logging trucks and outdoorspeople. The drive times were longer than she realized, and we were running behind. Kara was at the wheel, and the dirt road was slick with mud. I was terrified that we were going to slip, lose control, and careen into the grill of one of the oncoming logging trucks that barreled past at top speed.

"Please slow down," I said, more than once.

"We're fine," she said, determined to make this a fact.

The long drive was silent with tension. She knew the group was waiting for her, and I knew we could crash and crash badly. Mud spraying off the tires rained across the van's back windows, and I felt our grip on the road slip multiple times.

There's a turn to take from the Golden Road to reach Roll Dam, and there the road becomes less like a road and more like two tracks of exposed dirt with a wide strip of grass between them. The van jolted over the pockmarked and potholed path, and Kara kept the gas pedal pressed farther than she should have. I had just said, again, "I really think you should slow down" when the sickening sound of a front tire popping after it bashed into the edge of a hole in the road erupted beneath us.

Everything ended. Forward motion. Conversation. Hope of reaching the group. We sat in that silence for some immeasurable length of time before Kara started to cry.

"This is fine," I think I said, opening my door and sliding out until my hiking boots touched the ground. "I mean, it sort of has to be." I fought my way through the alders and undergrowth that pressed against the van until I stood in front of it. Kara joined me there, still crying, and we stood in the heat amid the crackling insects, regarding the deflated tire and leaning vehicle.

She was shaking her head, looking from the tire to the road ahead. I knew she was trying to guess how far we were from the group.

"Let's just get the spare out and change the tire. It won't take that long." I tried to rally some optimism, though optimism was never my natural habitat.

We fought our way back through the tangle of branches, reached the double doors at the rear of the van, and peered into a blank, empty hole where the spare was supposed to be.

Beneath the shirring green of birch leaves, we stood gaping at this fate. We were at least eight miles from the less-deserted Golden Road and three miles from the group. In theory we could sit here for days without seeing another person.

Kara spoke first. "You're going to have to go down the river with us."

This wasn't really possible. Even if we could walk to Roll Dam (and maybe we couldn't), I couldn't leave the van here. I had no gear with me. And the lack of cell service meant that I couldn't tell anyone why I didn't come back on schedule. "That's not an option" is likely all I said. "You know that's not an option."

My memory of these moments feels coated in glue. Everything is slowed down. Recollections of the scene feel weighed down with panic and uncertainty. The moist summer heat of my memory is oppressive and heavy. The distances we had traveled to reach this spot in the woods and this spot in our lives felt so enormous as to be visible from space. The camera of my memory pulls back on this scene and lets me see it from the vantage of the hot, distant sun.

I can't say how much time had gone by before we heard the impossible sound of an approaching vehicle. We froze, looking at each other in disbelief, and then a sunny yellow Jeep spilling over with robust young men rounded through the alders into full view. The Jeep, which reminded me of a Sport Walkman I had in the '90s, stopped when it came upon the blockade created by the van.

The driver, wearing sporty, outdoorsperson sunglasses, leaned out and said, "Flat tire?"

Faint with relief, we struggled our way to the front end of the sagging van. We confirmed the diagnosis in voices desperate for help.

"My parents are right behind us," he said. "Our dad will know what to do."

He maneuvered the Jeep around us and disappeared into the flora, heading the way we had come in, and within a minute another vehicle arrived ferrying into view an older man and woman. Their Subaru came to a stop and the man got out. "I'm Brad," he said. "Looks like you need some help."

From here, this story becomes one about the ways humans help each other with a combination of skill and luck. Brad and his wife heard the circumstances we faced and did all of the following: They drove us both to Roll Dam and delivered Kara to the surprised impatience of her waiting group, then returned with me to the van. Brad jacked up the vehicle, removed the tire, and delivered it to the impossibility of a store tucked down several more back roads. The store sold beer, potato chips, fishing lures and line, hunter-orange vests, and coffee. Miraculously, it also offered tire repair and other small mechanical necessities. Brad rolled the tire into the back, then we got back in the car. The couple took me to their hunting camp, where the group of young men had already arrived and were waiting. While the tire was being repaired, Brad's wife fixed me a tuna fish sandwich, and when it was time to go, she sent me with a bag of freshly baked oatmeal cookies. Brad took the tire and me back to the van. He put it in place, secured the lug nuts, and I eased the vehicle through the brush to the Golden Road, rolling into Millinocket as if nothing had happened at all. When I got home, I sent Brad's family a box of Lubec-made chocolates and added them to the learning center mailing list. They sent donations every year for the rest of my tenure as development director.

Kara had to slide her canoe into the river, leaving me in the hands of these kind strangers, without knowing if they were serial killers and whether I would make it home at all. Like so many other times across these early years of our relationship, we had to move with faith that, no matter how dire it looked, breakdowns were normal, problems could be solved, and at the end of each day we would be fine.

Two nights later, from the security and privacy of her tent on Gero Island, Kara pulled out the panda notebook and wrote:

Three more nights, love. We're on Gero Island. Chesuncook Village sits across the choppy water, alive in the moonlight. I wanted to write to you last night, and I couldn't. It would have all been fraught with worry. Today was a clear, sunny day. Our paddle down the Penobscot was smooth and relaxed. Across Chesuncook and along the island to find a site was work. There was a chop, and it took a lot of effort to get through it. It took a lot of effort to get through yesterday. The thought of having to leave you in the middle of nowhere, in the hands of strangers without me . . . well, I totally did not like that at all. I supremely did not like that. The other trip leader caught me crying as I packed the final things in my pack right after you left. Just as I bring out things in you, you bring out things in me. One is my usually reserved capacity to worry. I am still worrying. I want to call you so badly. I am praying to the universe that you are safe at home in your bed. I am so sorry for leaving you that mess to deal with. I hope it all went okay. It feels a little preemptive to write this. What if it didn't go okay? I love you so much, Penny. I'm totally worried. I want to know that you are safe. I've never felt this so profoundly before. Three more nights.

# Is This Parenting?

That same year, a therapist taught Abby how to act like a turtle.

"The idea is to teach Abby how to give herself some space," the therapist said to me in the waiting room of the community health center. It was a narrow room. At one end a collection of toys—a plastic kitchen, a bin full of action figures with missing limbs—waited for someone to play with them. "She needs to learn how to take herself out of a situation. To collect herself."

I had started bringing her to therapy when her anger had become pervasive and undeniable. When faced with the smallest slight, the tiniest reprimand, her face assumed a deep scowl—forehead furrowed beneath brown curly hair, mouth pressed into a hyphen, green eyes cold and narrow—and she stalked off to stomp and slam doors. She was a tiny-fisted, furious force in the home we now shared with Kara, my new partner.

And so she was instructed to be a turtle when she got angry. She was instructed to go inward—retreat into a shell—when she felt her anger get out of control. By being a turtle, she might survive my divorce. She might also survive whatever humiliations were sure to come from being in a small town and having her mother leave her father for a woman. She might survive my selfishness.

I drove her to counseling every week for a year. I drove her through all weather, through the darkest New England nights to these appointments. The drive took an hour each way.

Sometimes I dropped her off and tried to squeeze in grocery shopping or some other errand. Sometimes I brought a book and sat in the waiting room, trying to read. Sometimes I brought Owen, now four, and we went to McDonald's for a fruit cup or a carton of chocolate milk. He would slide into the bright-red booth and talk his incessantly cheerful talk. I leaned gratefully into his company. Always I spent those fifty minutes worrying about what was going on in that room with the puppets and the sand tray. What maternal crimes or shortcomings were being revealed?

She practiced being a turtle in the grocery store one day as the sliding glass doors whooshed shut behind us. She was angry at her little brother, and I watched her take herself to the far end of the store, near the meats and pickles, to collect herself.

I shopped for vegetables and bread but kept an eye on Abby. I put broccoli and strawberries into my cart while watching for her girly, purple coat and lavender boots. She stayed within sight but kept herself apart—stayed inside her shell. Owen stayed next to me, held onto the cart, and narrated the items on the shelves. Cereal. Syrup. Bread. We moved from aisle to aisle, and Abby appeared, dutifully, at each far end. We moved in orbits.

I wondered, "Is this parenting?"

A year after I moved into Kara's house, we started inviting John over for dinner now and then. We would spend a relatively pleasant evening around the dining room table, though I always drank too many glasses of wine to help me through the discomfort. But the kids loved it, loved having us all together, loved having their broken family repaired for at least a few hours.

Always, when the time came for him to leave, Abby stationed herself at her bedroom window to watch until his taillights disappeared behind the pines, and I had to hold her while she cried herself to sleep.

The book about parenting through a divorce didn't tell me that would happen.

It also failed to use these words: That shared custody means signing away half of their childhood. That my friends, in an effort to "not take sides," would work to become much closer to John than they had ever been before. That whatever my kids needed—a specific pair of shoes, a book, a Lego piece, a DVD, a doll, a sweater—would forever be at the other parent's house. That their very best drawings and paintings could only appear on the fridge at one house—that we would negotiate over these art works. That not one single form in the whole world—for dance class, for violin lessons, for therapy, for admittance to the emergency room, for book orders—acknowledges that kids might have more than one address and phone number. That my kids would learn that the phrase "I wish you and Daddy still lived together" would become the fast, direct road to extra television time, more sugar—whatever they wanted.

The parenting book made it sound like the challenges would all be internal, invisible, and my job was to ferret them out. The book made it sound like this happened all the time and that resilience was the only key. What the book left out was any consideration of the resilience of parents. There was no chapter on coping mechanisms for people like me. I had to write that chapter myself, and I did it every day, every time I counted to five over and over to calm myself or imagined writing scathing letters to the author of the book about divorce. "This isn't as easy as your book made it sound," I imagined typing to the smug writer. "My kids are probably going to be fine, but the effort might kill me. Why didn't you write about that?"

Six inches long, brown-bodied, lemon-colored spots—the salamander was the biggest I had ever seen. We found it in a deep pool of water next to our driveway on an early spring day. It was resting down there, in about eighteen inches of water, on brown, waterlogged leaves.

Abby leaned over for a closer look. Her face came close to the water's surface. "Do you think it's dead?"

We had been living in our new home since the previous autumn and had taken to the practice of walking on the weekends down our half-mile-long driveway. The dirt road rose and fell, winding its way through thick woods. Trees pressed in against the margins and shaded the way.

I poked lightly at the salamander with a long stick, and it wiggled in response. I fished it out and let it rest on the palm of my hand, its skin firm and slick like a sausage casing. We took turns holding it, touching it, turning it over to see its belly. It seemed sluggish and cold, as if it had just woken up from a sleep about the length of a winter. Once we had thoroughly examined it, we returned it to the watery hole. It swam purposefully back to the leaves at the bottom and hunkered down.

This pool of clear, springtime water was held in a round slice of concrete pipe about two feet tall. It was there, sitting on its end, collecting leaves, sticks, and rainwater, as it had been for an unknown number of years. It could have been a discarded piece of culvert. It might have been a cast-off remnant of someone's septic system. How it came to live next to our driveway was a mystery.

I felt uncertain about leaving the salamander there. The concrete walls were slick. I wondered if it could climb out, and if we were missing an opportunity to rescue it. I made the decision to leave it alone. This was another mistake. There were so many across this time. As I parented this complicated girl (and her less-complicated brother, who sometimes seemed, even at just four years old, to be parenting me right back), I often wished for some news from the future, even the near future. News from the following day or week would have been enough. Some reassurance that we would make it past even the very day we were in.

Two days later, on another walk, we returned to see how the creature was faring. Peering down through the water, we saw it there—just where we had left it—lying on its bed of slowly dissolving leaves. I nudged it with the stick. It did not wiggle this time, instead drifting stiffly off the leaves. It floated for just a moment, then landed on its side, its body now rigid. Legs, tail, and toes were splayed and inelastic.

Abby took a breath next to me. "He's dead," she half whispered.

Fishing the small corpse out of the water, I let it rest, once again, on the palm of my hand. The color of its skin had shifted from its previous rich, mocha brown to a color with shades of plums or eggplant. Its spots had faded and were now the color of dust.

"It's not the same one," Abby said. "It's a different color. This one is purple. The one we found was brown."

Her face was solemn, forehead knotted fiercely in concentration as she crouched next to me, studying the tiny remains in my hand. Coat open in the front, zipper dangling down and touching the slowly thawing ground, she was dressed for this early March day. Her pink, striped fleece hat was shoved down over her ears, brown curls escaping around the edges. Underneath her rubber boots, the frost on the crisp grass was yielding to the warmth and softening.

"You don't think it's the same one?" I asked her, uncertain, once again, of the best position to take.

She studied it for a moment longer. "It's a different one."

I considered this possibility while I thought about the moment that I had released this doomed animal into the frigid water in the concrete circle two days ago. I wished I had listened to the usually wrong voice in my head when it wondered if this salamander might appreciate being placed instead on the ground. There were so many mistakes.

"I guess it's possible," I answered her, turning the creature over. Its belly was darker too. Was the water too cold? Were the sides too slick to climb?

We left the dead salamander under some ferns next to the concrete tube and the water. As we stood and walked away, I considered doing what so many parenting books say to do: tell her the truth.

Instead, I said, "I wonder what happened to the brown one."

I held the newborn rodent curled in the palm of my hand. Its almost-microscopic toes were curled under its chin, and it bucked and squealed. With my other hand, I worked fast to pluck angry red ants from its soft, newborn fur—barely discernible from its soft, newborn skin. There were at least a dozen of them, biting and crawling in and out of the small folds made by the mouse's bent limbs. Before I tossed the ants into the grass, I savaged each by rolling it hard between my thumb and forefinger. Their legs, pincers, antennas, and firm bodies all balled together for just a moment before they became airborne. This vicious, well-organized army wanted to rip the newborn to pieces, and even as I worked to prevent that from happening, I wondered what the point was. My own shortcomings were so clear to me by this time that I had no illusions that I could change what was inevitable for this mouse. I could barely get my own babies through childhood intact.

Kara had found the mouse in the grass, next to the garden, abandoned by its mother and in the throes of dismemberment. I had swung into action because I needed to do right by somebody's babies, even if I couldn't get it right for my own. Those ants were easier to crush than the things that I feared were eating up my own kids. I could do this even if it didn't ultimately matter.

Once all the ants were removed, the animal stopped its tiny screams and relaxed into the folds of my palm. It was a mouse. Or a shrew. Or a vole. We had no idea, really, what kind of animal it was, how many days ago it had been born, or where its mother had gone. It lay there panting softly. Its eyes were clamped shut, too young to know daylight from night. We stood there, under a sinking July sun, next to tomato, kale, pumpkin, and chard plants—the rims of the leaves were lit from behind and shone like medals. We stood together, looking at the mouse, knowing it would die.

The area around our garden was lousy with tiny red ants, and they would immediately find the creature again if we put it back in the grass. If the mouse's mother was going to come back, she would have done so by now—she would not have given the ants enough time to swarm. I had tried, twice in the past, to feed abandoned baby mice through trimmed-down eyedroppers. Neither baby survived, and I had learned that a human can't replace a mother mouse. Even if I got in the car, made the trip to the store to buy a can of kitten milk, trimmed the eyedropper in exactly the right way, held the creature just so, and coaxed the life-giving fats and proteins into its mouth, it would die. Probably right there in my hand.

And there was Abby to consider. She was due to arrive from her dad's house the next morning. She was too keen, her senses too sharp for me to keep such a secret, and if she saw the mouse, saw me feeding it, she would become attached. There would be no way to craft a salamander-like lie around this. She would be there, watching it die, right next to me. And all of that, all the wasted time and gas and energy and tears, when the outcome was certain—what was the point? I was learning, or trying to, that there was relief in knowing my own limitations, the edges of my power. There was, somewhere, a list of the things I could fix, and this was not on it.

We made a nest out of a bowl and some hay and left the mouse in the garage overnight. We hoped it would all be over by morning.

It was not over in the morning. The mouse was exactly as we had left it: breathing, snuffling, warm, and entirely alive. We left it there in the garage while we went about our morning routines. We made coffee. We listened to the news. My kids came back from their dad's. After getting out of his car, they walked right by the garage, blissfully unaware. I checked on the mouse now and then as the morning went by. I thought about different ways to die. I had heard that starving to death is painful but that drowning can be worse. I wondered what it would be like to be crushed under the giant tire of a car. Would it be too fast to hurt? Was that possible? I thought about mercy and what that really looked like.

Kara and I stood in the kitchen, trying to decide what to do. Somewhere in the house, the kids were playing. I heard their laughter, their thumping noises. Kara pushed a strand of hair out of my eyes, and I straightened her glasses.

The right thing to do was to kill it fast. It was peanut-sized—fragile and soft. It barely had bones to break. I tried to place it on the continuum of the animal kingdom closer to insects and further from myself and my kids. I searched the area behind our garage—the place where we stack our wood and store our bikes—for some tool to do this job, trying to disassociate from its aliveness. I tried to think of it as a plant or a larval mosquito—something operating purely on genetic programming. Nothing that would be missed. I stepped over a pile of boards and thought about using one: flat and hard. I looked at our woodpile—each piece of firewood had an end that was flattened by the chain saw. Any one of them could do it. I tried to picture each item as it would look after I was done with this task. I pictured the blob of red and fur that would smear across one of these surfaces. It had to be something that I didn't have to clean off.

I saw the cinder block at the base of the woodpile.

Something took over. Some sort of focus—a certainty. I wasn't gifted with any sort of moral quiet. No voices spoke to me saying, *You are merciful, you are kind, you are sparing this animal a much more painful end.* What seized me was closer to the feeling of a deadline. The feeling that something has already gone on too long. The feeling that even though I did not bring this situation on myself, it was mine to manage, like so many other situations I was in. There were so many bad decisions I had made, so many wrong turns, so much damage that I believed I was inflicting—I had to do this right. And it had to be now.

One-handed, I lifted the cinder block, walked behind the woodpile, placed the mouse on a flattened spot on the ground, lifted the cinder block in the air, and brought the flat side down on the mouse as firmly and decisively as I could. I then stepped on it, pressing it farther down with my boot. It was as if lifting the cinder block, walking, putting the mouse down, raising the block into the air, and smashing it down were all one singular motion. One smooth, hard decision.

I lifted the block slightly, needing to know if I had finished the job. Even if this turned out to be the wrong thing to do, I needed to know that I had done it right. The mouse was there, surrounded by a halo of red and wetness. I dropped the block again and staggered away from the woodpile. The shock of what I had just done pressed in and made me dizzy, made it hard to keep my legs under me.

Abby emerged from the house and ran across the lawn to me, her brown curls bouncing. She was long-legged and smiling. Her arms, lithe and tan, wrapped around my waist. She leaned her head against my chest. I felt her warmth and let the light of her smile into my body, let it put my legs back underneath the rest of me. I felt the shaking subside.

When the puppet show was over and we parted ways, Abby stood next to my car and watched her father and his new girlfriend walk across the parking lot. She stood, motionless, and watched them get into the car, watched the headlights flick on, heard the engine start. She stood there, in the darkening, thickening evening summer fog, in the grass with thick coastal dew already collecting on its tips, and watched. She wore her winged unicorn costume. Its hood, the unicorn's head, covered her own. From behind, I watched this small, fuzzy, hooded girl, with crinkly, iridescent wings, with ears standing up on top of the hood, with the horn pointed toward the treetops, as the night started to get dark. She had two blue balloons tied to the zipper of her costume, and they floated silently, not moving, just above her unicorn's horn. I could not see her face. That picture, of this small, shimmering unicorn, standing stock still with unmoving blue balloons over her horn, serves up evidence of our failures. Her grief bobbed above her head next to the balloons in the blue light of dusk as she watched her father's car pull slowly away. The trees and grass and asphalt and sky became bluer and bluer as the minutes passed. I tried to coax her into my car, but she wanted to watch until she couldn't see his car anymore. She wanted to watch us move away from each other.

When she finally allowed me to guide her into my car, she became a weeping, devastated unicorn with blue balloons, and as I drove us home through the cobalt fog, my hands gripping the wheel, straining to see the road, I wept too. It was one of those foggy nights when putting the headlights on high didn't make the route home any clearer. We all drove into that fog.

Our driveway is a long, wooded approach. It's several minutes of gravel under the tires, trees lining both sides of my peripheral vision, and then the house appears at the far end of the clearing. In the dark and fog of that night, it was just a large, black shape. There was a single light left on in an upstairs window—Abby's room. She had left on the daisy-shaped lamp that served as her night light. Made of molded plastic, it had pink, bulbous petals and a perfect green circle in its center. The daisy was intended to hang on a wall, but we kept it on the windowsill instead, leaning against the glass. That night, from across the field and through the fog, it appeared to us as a glowing, pink flower floating two stories up in the night.

I heard Abby humming a song behind me. We drove toward that light.

# PART 3

# Tight Margins and Powerful Strangers

Maybe I reheated a red pepper and broccoli stir fry in the microwave. Or maybe I fluffed salad greens with tofu cubes, artichokes, and that Moosewood vinaigrette I was making at home every week. Perhaps we pulled out egg salad and spread it across thick slices of bread or crackers. Whatever we ate that day, we were at work, and it was lunchtime.

Kara and I sat at one of the round, blue tables in the room that was both community space and office kitchen (and, when needed, a classroom, lobby, reception area, or movie theater). The day's news played—audio only—from the tiny speaker of a laptop. Down in Augusta, in the austere state capitol chambers, the senate was voting.

We listened to the roll call. Each senator, "Aye" or "Nay." With a healthy 25 percent margin, the bill won 20–15 in the senate and 89–58 in the house, and the governor signed it. Just like that. With this vote, the state of Maine repealed its 1997 ban on same sex marriage, and it was the first state to have done so in the legislature rather than at the ballot box.

I put my hand on Kara's, next to our plates of salad or warmed-up pizza, and our eyes met, and we smiled. Our coworkers cheered across their respective plates of lunch. We lifted spoons and forks, laughed, and Kara and I, caught up in the revelry, grinned but did not answer well-intentioned questions about when the wedding might be. We finished lunch, did the dishes, then everyone went back to work, but we all knew what would happen next.

I had been political for my entire adult life. In 1990, when I was a senior in college, Ralph Nader delivered a speech on my campus, and while I can't tell you exactly what he said, he lit me on fire with the need to be involved. Regardless of how I would feel about Nader in later years, his speech that day led me to work for the nonprofit he started, MASSPIRG, and from there I worked on the re-election campaign for U.S. Representative Tom Andrews (once voted the most progressive member of Congress), and from there I worked for a citizen action organization that trained me as a lobbyist, and from there I went back to school to get a master's degree in public policy.

In other words, nothing about what happened next in Augusta surprised me. Laws are expressions of power and privilege, and it was not news in 2009 that neither power nor privilege had taken up residence in LGBTQ+ families.

Before the repeal of the ban could take effect, the Maine Christian Civic League filed their petition to take the matter to referendum. The state put enactment on hold until the voters had had their say on our right to be together, and though I knew politics, I had never felt this particular flavor of pain. As a longtime cis, straight-identifying person, I had enjoyed the benefits of our socially conservative, narrow understanding of what qualifies as a legitimate relationship. Existing on the spectrum of outness is a series of personal decision points, but it's also political. It's politics with a small "p" when you are asked at a party if you're married, and you don't know how to answer the question in anything less than a paragraph. It's the other kind of Politics when the legitimacy of your family is quite literally on the ballot.

Their side was "Vote Yes!" in support of repealing the law, and ours was "Vote No!" in favor of leaving it in place. The Nation of Referendum Questions is situated on the Planet of Double Negatives, and nobody ever seems able to word these things in a way that allows for campaign slogans that make sense to voters, but that's not why we lost that referendum. A campaign funded almost entirely by out-of-state individuals proudly turned back marriage rights by a six-point margin. Campaign records reveal that one guy named Sean Fieler, who lived in Connecticut, donated over a million dollars to keep me from getting married. It cost him four dollars per vote. I don't know what to do with that information.

# Across the Bridge

*In memory of Charlie Howard*

Three years later, in the summer of 2012, Kara and I walked down the middle of Main Street in Calais, Maine. We were two people in a contingent of seventy walking in full-on rainbow garb, showing up to make a statement about equality. This was not a pride parade. This was a small-town, summer parade, and our group was in the lineup after the Kiwanis club and before the bagpipe band from Canada. The issue of same sex marriage was back on the Maine ballot, this time to repeal the repeal of marriage rights. Put more simply, the question said this: "Do you want to allow the State of Maine to issue marriage licenses to same-sex couples?" The statewide campaign had urged supporters to organize visibility opportunities like this one. We were urged to march, to be seen, to make noise.

As we walked, Kara held a plastic rainbow flag in her left hand. It snapped and unfurled over and over in front of the crowd. I reached for her right hand, but she pulled away. That trip to Provincetown was years behind us—a small bright spot somewhere on the timeline over our shoulders. Here at home, she couldn't be seen holding hands with a woman, even when we were wearing our colors, marching in a parade behind the marriage equality float. Her job now was as a high school teacher, and she feared that someone—one of her students, the superintendent, a conservative parent—might see. She pressed her lips together firmly and let her eyes go soft in apology as she pulled her hand away. I couldn't be upset. She was right. We weren't that kind of out.

The parade was part of the International Festival—the weekend when the border towns of St. Stephen, New Brunswick, and Calais, Maine, celebrated their goodwill toward each other by erecting a beer tent, hiring a band, and inviting vendors to line both sides of both main streets. The walls of trailers selling sausage sandwiches and cotton candy were broken only by the bridge spanning the St. Croix River marking the border with Canada. On the north side of that bridge, gay people had marriage rights. On our side, we had to march with the Shriners and the spangly girls from the dance school with their inappropriately sexualized moves. We were marching in parades all over the county that summer, trying to be visible, trying to be less scary.

A young blonde woman and her equally blond boyfriend marched next to us, brazenly holding hands as we passed the storefronts and the movie theater. With their free hands, they waved rainbow flags. While marching in support of our love, they blissfully celebrated their own.

The parade threaded between booths selling fried dough, crabmeat rolls, jewelry, and dream catchers imported from China. My daughter wore a full-sized rainbow flag as a cape and held hands with her friend Ruby as they handed out candy to kids along the parade route. At their age, girls could hold hands. Ruby wore a canvas bag slung across her chest and judiciously distributed brightly wrapped Tootsie Rolls, lollipops, and Starlight mints.

I had talked to my kids about the campaign like this: *Some people think that a woman shouldn't be able to marry another woman and a man shouldn't be able to marry another man.* I had carefully languaged the topic to keep the danger somewhere out there in the world, not in our home. During some particular car ride, when I drove while listening to the radio, some anti-gay news item prompted me to say, "Give me a break" out loud. Abby asked what I was talking about, and I said, "Oh, it's nothing. Some people just don't like gay people very much I guess." A mile or so went by before she said, "Mommy, what's a gay person?" and I realized how much work I had not done.

Our float was a white pickup truck, adorned with flags and banners, pulling a trailer of three television sets tall enough so everyone could see them and rolling a video composed of still images of families—two moms with their arms draped around each other and their children, two dads staring tenderly at their infant, families doing all the things that families do. A catchy pop song called "We're Marching On" blasted out of tall speakers, and the entire contraption was followed by our group wearing bright-colored clothing, waving flags, bouncing beach balls, smiling, and waving. Kids along the parade route, whatever their parents were thinking, loved us. We were a kaleidoscope. A jukebox. A prism in the sun.

I want to say this: even a parade with music, beach balls, glitter, gaudy plastic flower garlands, and rainbows everywhere is not fun if your right to exist as a family is something you have to march for. I don't love parades. I don't love crowds or blaring fire engines, silly string or clowns, Shriner go-karts or waving politicians. I didn't want to go. I didn't want to hand out rainbow snap bracelets or throw packages of Skittles into the crowd. I wanted to be at home pulling weeds from our vegetable garden or taking a nap. We were there because it was required of us.

I positioned myself in the group so I could keep an eye on Abby and Ruby but also see Kara. Some people in the crowd clapped for us, and I thanked them with a nod and a smile while keeping the pavement moving under my feet. Others were harder to read. As they checked their watches or stared at their feet, I tried to imagine what they might be thinking and tried not to be afraid. Still others were easy to read: their message was ugly as they glared directly into my eyes. One man frowned with deep, droopy jowls and gave me an emphatic thumbs down. One woman hissed at me, "Bunch of queers" as we went past.

Even though I had once volunteered for the effort to stop the turnpike widening, gone door-to-door to campaign for better recycling laws, lobbied to protect victims of medical malpractice, made phone calls to fundraise for universal health care, and generally lived an activist's life out loud, this was different.

If someone scowled, slammed the door, or hung up it bounced off me. I could shrug and agree to disagree with someone who favored more pavement, but it was harder when the issue was my right to exist at all.

I don't remember if it was for the Vote No campaign (against the ballot measure that would repeal the new marriage equality law) or for the Vote Yes campaign (in favor of the ballot measure that would enact the good law) that we threw a fundraiser in our garage or which effort had the orange signs, but I know that I never did put a bumper sticker on my car. I know it was during the campaign to repeal the good law that I learned how many times a Honda CRV must run over a lawn sign to make it stay down for good (three times, and the middle swipe must be taken in reverse). Our lawn was too remote for a sign that was better placed somewhere visible, so we never had one.

Our feet trod pavement just ninety-five miles from the spot where Charlie Howard was murdered in 1984 in Bangor, Maine, for being gay. Three teenage boys, ages fifteen to seventeen, saw Charlie walking with his boyfriend, so they pursued him, beat him, and threw him into the Kenduskeag Stream, where he drowned. Later, the boys told the police they had just wanted to "beat up a faggot." They were tried as juveniles, and each was released at age twenty-one.

It mattered that this murder was almost thirty years before this parade and that it was a different time, but only sort of. I did not fear for my life on that summer day in 2012 walking in the middle of a pack in daylight with a police presence. We are meant to take that as progress, which it is, but also isn't.

In some places along the parade route, entire groups of people clapped. Cheered, even. Gave us the thumbs up. Came off the curb to high-five us. The glaring, scowling, watch-checking people had to realize that it was the people standing on both sides of them who were cheering. I hoped that they started to feel just a little bit alone. I hoped that, somewhere deep within their will, a crack started to form, or a question. "Is it just me?"

Our group had just passed a used car dealership when the clouds broke open with rain that soaked our flags and banners. We scrambled to cover the television sets with blue tarps. The rain lasted only a minute, then ceased, but dark clouds crowded over the downtown. The white truck rounded the corner by the park, and we reached the end of the parade route just as rumbles of thunder rolled in from across the river. The group quickly folded the banners and deflated the balloons.

A few minutes later Kara, the kids, and I stood in line at Burger King, our clothes still damp, and studied the backlit menus. Our rainbow gear—flags, snap bracelets, flowery leis—was all stowed in the back of the car. In regular, rainbow-free clothing, we were covert again.

Behind us in line, a young straight couple had their arms over each other's shoulders. Her hand was on his chest, her head nuzzled up against his neck. It was as though they had finished making love, hopped out of bed, and headed straight to Burger King instead of just rolling over and lighting a cigarette. His hand strayed to her rear end, and they giggled and kissed. Right there in the Burger King.

I glanced at Kara to find her looking directly at me, and we settled for a long moment of green eyes locked with blue. She kept her hands in her pockets.

We won the 2012 referendum, but it's not like it made anything simple. In 2011 Kara and I got married in Massachusetts, then were not married anymore once we drove home. In 2012, at the whim of the electorate, we were married again, but not when we filed our federal taxes because nothing had changed at the national level. In 2015, with my kids in the back seat of that same Honda CRV, while we headed south down 95 to meet Kara in western Maine, where we would begin a family vacation involving a three-day drive to Michigan, my phone vibrated with notifications for five miles before I looked at it and learned that the Supreme Court had reached a 5–4 decision in *Obergefell v. Hodges*, making same sex marriage the law of the land. I came to understand that one vote by one Supreme Court justice (equaling 20 percent of the nine seated judges) had turned me into a very different citizen at Exit 1 than I was at Exit 20. I saw my Exit 20 self—the self that had tossed salad greens or heated up pizza and listened to the votes of powerful strangers—in the rearview mirror. I changed the station on the radio to something the kids liked, rolled the window down to smell the summer air, eased my way around a camper from Massachusetts, and drove toward the state line.

# I Dreamed I Was at the Funeral of an Activist

Hundreds of stooped, hunched people gathered to mourn the murder of the gay rights activist—someone famous. The crowd spread across an unripe, spring lawn, over the crest of a hill, and curved around the soggy edge of a lake. In front, someone spoke, and in the odd logic of dreams, the killer was in the front row, agonized by the act he had committed. His long face was contorted, and he pressed his flattened palms into his cheeks. He looked at the sky, searching for some answer.

I walked to the front of the group, made uneasy eye contact with the killer, and approached the white, closed, shiny-handled casket. It rested on the shoulders of six people I deeply loved.

The first shot took out one of the pall bearers. It came from somewhere across the lawn. The person I loved crumpled to the ground, deflated, blood pooling around his feet. A second shot. Reality started to creep in. The third shot tore through my left shoulder.

"I'm being shot in a mass shooting," I thought. Unspeakable, unknowable dream pain rippled through my body, and I fell to the grass. "This is so American."

# Waxwings

When I was a kid, maybe twelve years old, my family's cat made three trips in one day across the yard to someplace in the woods where baby birds were falling like rain. The cat carried three fluffy, disheveled chicks, one at a time, each alive and flailing, into our house and deposited them at my mother's feet.

We scooped up those babies, no bigger than fat strawberries, and made a nest for them in a cardboard box. They were impossibly light with smoky-gray down and slate-colored beaks. We kept their box in the claw-footed tub in the bathroom with a window screen over the top to keep the cats out. Within an hour, one of the three was dead, probably wounded somehow in the jaws of the cat. The surviving birds thrust their open mouths upward whenever they sensed our presence. For two days, we poked smashed bunchberries into their gullets. We fed and fed and fed. Their tiny heads peeped and bobbed, demanding more, and then they dozed.

We held them in our cupped hands, warming them. We stroked the tops of their heads, smoothed their feathers. We would later find out that they were cedar waxwings, a bird I had never seen before and would not see again for decades. I imagined their confusion at this crazy turn of events. I wondered if they were thinking about their nest. What was it like to have one, reliable home and to know nothing else until, abruptly, everything in the world became unfamiliar? I worried that they missed their mother.

One afternoon, several years after I had moved out of the house I still owned with John, I came by to pick up some things that had been left behind. John's new girlfriend was moving in, and whatever I might have left in the corners and closets had to go.

Abby, nine years old, asked me, "Mama, do you want to see my super-secret hideout in the backyard?"

I followed her around the outside of the house. Her curls bounced against her shoulders as she pranced ahead of me. She had grown so much taller over the last year, her legs, arms, and body elongating like the young cherry trees in the backyard that John and I had planted on our wedding day eleven years earlier.

Cedar waxwings are found only in North America, and they are monogamous. Their heads are the color of coffee, caramel, brown sugar glaze on old-fashioned donuts, pinecones, and toffee. The color, as it makes its way down the length of their sleek bodies, shifts subtly into the color of pewter, cedar bark, or winter skies. With crests atop their heads, and sharp black beaks, they look like blue jays dressed down. They wear black masks. The boys come with flashy red spots on the tips of their wing feathers, which they show off to the girls. Their tail feathers are either bright yellow or orange, depending on what type and color of berries their parents gorged on.

They are modern couples. They work together to build their nests, and both mom and dad take care of the kids. They also have harsh boundaries, as it turns out, as they care for the fledglings for only a couple of weeks before introducing them to flight. Once this feat is mastered and the nest is empty, the couple will start all over and, if there is time, raise another batch in the same year. In this haste, a few babies might be forced out of the nest too early, make the jump too soon, and end up in the mouth of a house cat.

Cedar waxwings are generous and romantic. When courting, the blushing couple will lounge in a treetop, passing a flower petal, a piece of pinecone, or an insect back and forth between them. The item is offered and accepted, from one black beak to the other and back again, over and over. If a group of waxwings are all interested in a single clump of berries, they will form a line on the drooping twig and pass berries, beak to beak, to the birds in the back, so that everyone gets enough.

Abby led me through the backyard, which was lusher and greener than I remembered. I had not been behind the house for at least three years. The forsythia bush that I had planted as a sapling a decade earlier now spanned six feet and had rocketed upward to be taller than I was. The arborvitae trees—also small shrubs when we planted them along the property line to protect us from view of the neighbors—were now a formidable wall of cedar. Likewise for the poplar hybrids, chosen for their quick-growing properties, which had shot up and leafed out like leggy young horses.

Abby rounded the forsythia bush, hunkered down on the ground, parted its dangling branches, and disappeared inside. From inside the bush, she said, "Look in here."

I crouched and squinted into the hole. The bush's branches rose from a central clump, then arched overhead and drooped earthward, leaving a nine-year-old-girl-sized space inside. She sat in there, knees pulled up to her chin, bare feet tucked close to her bottom, grinning at me. Spots of shade and sunlight dappled her skin. "It's perfect in here," she said.

I nodded, leaning in farther to see more of the inside. "It's completely perfect."

Behind me, the magnolia and plum and cherry trees John and I had planted together swayed in the breeze, whispering to me, wondering where I've been. They were at least twice as tall as I remembered. Abby came out of her super-secret hideout, took me by the hand, and gave me a tour of the backyard. This is the swing set. This is the sand box. This spot was a garden once. She did not know that I had chosen the swing set and arranged for its delivery or that I loaded two hundred pounds of bags of play sand into my car and drove it home. I had planted and tended that garden. If I still lived there, it would still be a patch of tomatoes, lettuce, peppers, and basil instead of a square of scraggly weeds.

On the third day of the waxwing babies being without their mother, we set the cardboard box on the deck overlooking the backyard. A screen covered the opening to allow the sun in but to keep the babies from escaping or a predator from climbing in. We imagined that the sun and air might feel good to these small, feral animals who did not belong in a box in our bathtub. Their security had been stolen from them, and we could not give it back, but we could at least let them see the sky.

In their box, under the screen, the babies chirped and rustled. While we went about our day, our eating, working, playing, and talking, the mother waxwing arrived from somewhere, fluttering on top of the screen, peering through it into the darkness of the box, tilting her bird head to get a better look. I imagine her now, having spent frantic, grief-filled days crisscrossing the forest looking for her babies, hearing their voices, and rushing toward them through the smells of humans, cats, and dogs, only to find them in a dark, human-scented cave, trapped by this strangeness. Could she sense that the missing one was gone forever?

She flew away, and we yanked the screen off the box. She came back and landed, her tiny bird-toes scratching and gripping the box's raw edge, with a single berry and thrust it into the waiting mouth of a baby. This began a series of trips from forest to box; each trip brought one berry, one unit of relief, one click toward normalcy.

Mothers of every species are skilled planners: we are all thinking about the next five things that must happen. While the mother bird was delivering berries to the gaping mouths of her brood, she was also thinking about the approaching night and worrying how she would ever move the babies across the gulf between the box and her nest. Because mothers are problem-solvers, she spent the afternoon teaching those babies to fly. She lured them first to the edge of the box, then to the edge of the deck, then into the air.

Over and over, from their perch at the edge of the planking, hearing their mother calling from the trees at the edge of the yard, they hurled themselves into the air with a wild, unpatterned flapping and plummeted to the lawn. My mother and I spent that same afternoon making trips off the deck to pluck the babies from the ground and return them to the planking after each failed attempt at flight. Everyone—mother waxwing, mother human, babies, and I—was determined that this should work, and before the sun set, the three birds were singing to each other from the tops of trees out of sight from the dark box, the screen, and the bathtub.

It's only now that I recognize myself in that mother bird, for the way she yanked everything familiar away from her babies and then showed up to fix it later.

When it was time for me to leave my old house that day, Abby skipped alongside my car as I eased down the driveway. She pranced the length of the lawn, her bare feet lifting and landing in the grass. She knew better than to run into the road, and I knew she would stop at the driveway's mouth, but I was scared for both of us anyway. What if she didn't stop? What if she flew into the road, into oncoming danger? I drove so slowly it was like I was barely moving. My window was down, and she was laughing in the face of this ever-unfolding abandonment.

When we reached the edge of the road, we both stopped, and she turned to wave. She was smiling, jumping up and down. I blew her a kiss, and my vision blurred as she blew one back. I drove onto the road, leaving her there with her super-secret forsythia nest.

Though I would go on to feed chickadees from my hand, witness bald eagles hunting from the air, fall in love with the pushy boldness of blue jays shoveling seed out of my feeders, feel transfixed by shimmering hummingbirds, dazzling goldfinches, red-winged blackbirds perched on drooping reeds, and the fog-colored dignity of catbirds, the cedar waxwing remained one of my favorites, though I didn't see another one until I was thirty-eight years old looking through Kara's kitchen window at the highbush cranberry growing just on the other side of the glass. It was morning, I was pouring coffee, and the branches were crowded with waxwings quietly feasting, fluttering, and handing each other berries.

# Squaring the Circle

JUNE 2011

The nylon walls of the tent glowed like cobalt metal, hot in the sun, disorienting me. I rolled over, rustling sleeping bag against camping pad. Kara's side of the tent was empty. I extracted my arms from my bag and dug my watch from the tent pocket. It was 9:30. Had I ever slept past 6:00 in a tent?

"Kara?" I said into the empty tent.

Her voice came from the other side of the nylon wall. "I'm out here." She set her metal coffee cup down on the picnic table, making a familiar, dull thunk.

"I can't believe I slept this late," I said, unzipping the tent door. How had she opened it without waking me? "What are you doing?" I inchwormed my way onto the sandy Cape Cod ground.

She sat at the picnic table, a paperback opened in front of her and a cup of coffee next to her elbow. Her hair was down, falling over her shoulders. She was in the T-shirt and the flannel pants she wore as pajamas. "Good morning."

It was Saturday morning, and we were on the flexed arm of Cape Cod with nothing to do for two days except run out the clock on the mandatory two-day waiting period before we could exchange wedding vows. We had arrived in Wellfleet the afternoon before, just in time to apply for a license. While Massachusetts allowed couples like us to get married, they required that all couples take a couple of days to make sure. This requirement is paternalistic and insulting, but we got over it when we realized it would force us to take a long weekend on the Cape.

I sat across from Kara at the table and tried to climb out of the foggy stupor of oversleeping. She poured me a cup of coffee. I put my hands around it, blinking in the full light of midmorning. "I can't believe I slept so late." Pine needles stuck to the bottoms of my bare feet under the table. The sand was warm.

"I know. Me neither," she said, her eyes returning to her book.

I spun my body to rest my back against the table. My feet rested on the sandy dirt near one of the tent stakes. The tent was new—a special purchase for this weekend. Kara and I had come to the relationship with our own histories of camping gear. I had an old gray REI tent that I had hauled all over the White Mountains, and she had a blue Sierra Designs model that she had lived in, essentially, during her expedition-based grad school days. We loved those pieces of gear as pieces of our own histories—our very selves—but recognized the need to zip new memories into the interior of a new space defined by slippery fabric walls. Our new tent, forever known as the wedding tent, was a long, narrow Sierra Designs product, blue and silvery gray, with an easy-to-set-up system of clips and skinny, folding poles.

The afternoon before, we had pushed open the heavy door to Wellfleet City Hall and walked the length of a polished, gleaming hallway in exactly the sort of building one imagines to be an old New England city hall. The clerk stood, unsmiling, as we pushed our paperwork across the counter to her. Kara and I exchanged glances. Was the clerk unsmiling because she was at work and had to deal with the public all day? Was the person she served just before us a complete jerk? Or was she homophobic? Was her unreadable and unremarkable expression about us?

It didn't matter. She signed and stamped what she needed to sign and stamp, and we were released. On Monday morning the justice of the peace we found online would meet us at the beach, and we would wear the silver jewelry we brought with us, hold hands, and say our vows, all regardless of what the perhaps-grumpy city clerk thought about it.

In the meantime, we had to find and buy outfits. We had to wander, shop for rainbow-colored trinkets, buy a Wellfleet refrigerator magnet, and slurp oysters and beer from a second-story balcony overlooking the shore. We had to find a used bookstore and stagger out under the weight of armloads of titles, then find a vineyard with tastings.

I stretched my legs straight in the increasing sunlight, drank my coffee, and listened to Kara turn a page of her book behind me. This memory of sleeping late, of not even hearing the tent zipper or the coffee being made, speaks to me now of the deep fatigue I carried into our early marriage and of my muscles' need to let go and relax. To catch up on the restorative elixir of doing nothing. Of standing still. It would become difficult for us, in later years, to achieve this stasis. The "us" of the future would pay for yoga retreats, books about meditation, mindfulness classes. We would spend money on comfortable furniture for indoors and outdoors and create what we referred to as our "outdoor living space" on the deck of our house. We would try to find the mind space of stillness that came so easily in those early days of our togetherness. Moments of bone-level peace would always arrive, but over the coming decade they would be further and further spaced. That weekend in Wellfleet stands out to me now as a counterfact to much of the busyness, projects, parenting, and living that was yet to come.

If one were to trace the origins of abstract painting, one would find this story somewhere in the research: One day, Russian-born artist Wassily Kandinsky walked into his studio to find an unfamiliar painting on his easel. It was unrecognizable and strange "but of extraordinary beauty, glowing with inner radiance." He stared at it for some time before realizing it was one of his own paintings upside-down. The revelation was so startling that it ended his relationship with concrete subjects and launched an exploration into line, shape, and color.

Among art historians, there is some disagreement about who made the first abstract painting, but there is no dispute over

Kandinsky's subsequent exploration into circles and colors and his influence over abstractions of the future. His paintings of concentric circles are famous: brightly colored shapes stacked atop one another like bullseyes. Interestingly, these messy stacks of circles are each confined within a square, and the squares are arranged in a grid of rows and columns. According to Kandinsky, "The circle is the synthesis of the greatest oppositions. It combines the concentric and the eccentric in a single form and in equilibrium." "Concentric" and "eccentric" refer to movement and production of force: concentric motion creates force by moving one way, and eccentric movement produces force by moving the other. The comparison seems most often used in the context of how we use our muscles—we contract and lengthen, but I doubt Kandinsky was talking about bicep curls. It seems he was imagining a circle—or a sphere—the way I had regarded the infinity symbol on the credit union sign: a glowing, ethereal thing held in place by thick fog. Concentric forces outside Kandinsky's circles keep them from expanding infinitely while eccentric forces put their shoulders against the curve to prevent an implosion. I think of him there in Russia, near the turn into the 1900s, selecting colors from a wooden palette and pushing them into circles on a canvas, then selecting the next color. My imagination then goes too far and thinks of him in eyeglasses with circular frames, sitting on a round stool beneath a circular moon and perched atop his spot on the circumference of the planet.

But why did Kandinsky put his tremulous, almost-kinetic circles inside of squares? Why did he construct a rigid grid in which to spin his eccentric magic?

On Monday morning, our muscles liquid from the weekend of moving like slow currents, Kara and I packed up the wedding tent, coffee maker, camp stove, and sleeping bags, then drove to the campground's bathroom building. Wooden doors to the stalls banging closed behind other campers, we dressed in our finery to the sound of toilets flushing and air dryers. I wore a loose black tank top and a white wrap-around layer on top of it—like a shawl with arms. My crinkly, silvery skirt came all the way to my feet. Kara had found a white tank top, shirred in the front, made to look like it wrapped around her body, and a pair of neutral-toned pants. She also found a dark gray wrap-around top to cover her shoulders. If not for our skin tones, our eyes and hair, we could have been a black-and-white photo in those clothes. In the campground bathroom, using the mirrors over the row of sinks, we combed our hair.

Within hours, we would be married. Before the end of the day, we would cross the bridge into Maine, where we would no longer be married.

It sounds like a logic question from a standardized test. The ones that ask questions like, "A farmer needs to get a fox, a goose, and a bag of grain across a river in his boat, which will only carry one animal or item at a time. He can't leave the fox with the goose or the goose with the bag of grain. How does he get them across the river?" Mine goes like this: "She has had three weddings but only been married twice. She was married in June but not married until the following January. She is married in nine states but not the other forty-one. Is she married or not?"

I gathered some of my hair and braided it down the back, then slid earrings into place. My feet were in sandals, but I knew I would kick them off and be barefoot for the ceremony. Squinting at myself through the steam on the mirror, I decided I was ready and then turned to look at my bride. Standing there on the concrete, under fluorescent lighting, within the painted white walls of the bathroom, we could hear someone taking a shower. Someone else turned on the hand dryer. Two teenage girls walked by the screen door, laughing, and one of them carried a basin of dirty dishes. Sunlight through the windows created blocks of lit-up cement by our feet. Kara had not yet put on her wrap, and her shoulders were bare. She wore her sport sandals, nylon straps cinched down. I stopped breathing for just a moment as I considered the magnitude of what we were going to do. It had settled in over the mandatory waiting period. This moment, with the mixture of light from the windows and the buzzing overheads, was to become our forever. Her long hair was down, and it draped across her bare shoulders, making me think of all the times I had moved her hair to the side so I could put my mouth on those same shoulders. Outside, someone honked a horn. I checked my watch.

JULY 2002

A dozen hammers whacked against nail heads, driving them into the blond cedar planks of our deck. Our oldest friends, young nieces and nephews, siblings and parents, aunts and uncles crouched on the deck, diligently pounding in galvanized steel nails, securing the decking in place. They had been working since midmorning and would finish just after lunch. This was my wedding with John.

It was one of those July days in Maine that can make people poetic about the coast. The sun was out, salt was in the air, and there was enough breeze to keep the bugs down. Tall poplar trees lining our property caught the wind, and their leaves spun and whirred like applause. Grasses and wildflowers in the front yard softly bowed, showing the light sides of their stalks and leaves. My friend Carol wandered through that small field, wearing a straw, summer hat, collecting wildflowers for my bouquet. Her skirt gently rippled around her knees.

I was anti-wedding. I had worked as a photographer and spent many weekends at peoples' weddings, trying to capture the moments that brides imagined would happen but rarely did. I had seen too many unity candles, awkward first dances, hungover groomsmen giving ill-conceived toasts, and grooms who seemed surprised by all that unfolded in front of them, as if it had all occurred through magic. I had given up hours of my life trying to settle brides amid oceans of poofy tulle, trying to coax a natural smile or at least some semblance of composure. Brides, in my experience, were miserable creatures—stressed out by the details, having no fun, reduced to merely enduring the day.

It was perhaps prophetic that the cards we mailed to friends and family invited them to a "big deck-building party" rather than to a wedding; inserted in much smaller font was the notice that at some point during the big party, we would get married. I was anti-wedding, but I may also have been forecasting something about how I really felt about this marriage. It was like I was sneaking in the back door of the commitment, hoping it wouldn't be a big deal. This first wedding counted because it was with a man. I will not ever get over the strange irony that this marriage, through the simple luck of our differing anatomies, came with all the associated recognitions and tax breaks.

When I think about it now, I think about Burkard Polster's assertion that anyone who walks the length of a Mobius strip will "feel perfectly fine all the way throughout the trip" but will "come back strange." I look up "coming full circle" in *Merriam Webster*, which explains it as "a series of developments that lead back to the original source, position or situation or to a complete reversal of the original position."

Is that how Kandinsky thought about it? When he did not recognize his own upside-down canvas and took it in as abstract shapes and colors in conversation with each other instead of the barn or canyon or bottle-with-apples he had begun, did he return to that spot in his studio a different person once he flipped the canvas right-side-up? It seems he did. He left that moment wanting to stack circles that shared a middle point one atop the other just to see what would happen. After he said what he did about circles existing in the sweet tension between concentricity and eccentricity, he added this: "Of the three primary forms, it [the circle] points most clearly to the fourth dimension."

Walking the circumference of a process or the tightrope of a timeline, whether it's a circle or something weirder and less predictable, may bring you back to the place you started, but you won't know that until you get there. And you might feel fine the whole trip—or you might not—but when you arrive back where you started, you are changed by the journey. You are more tired. You are older. You have seen some shit. You have confronted your mistakes but maybe made friends with their echoes.

Circle (sphere), square (cube), and triangle (tetrahedron) are the three primary forms, and I don't know why Kandinsky felt that it's the circle that is most likely to evoke the fourth dimension. In fact, there isn't clarity about what, exactly, the fourth dimension is. To mathematicians it's something so complicated and abstract that I have read about it over and over and still can't make sense of this particular ordering of words I already know. But Albert Einstein said that the fourth dimension is time, and we all know what that is. It's the stuff we burn through like it's as infinite as the digits in pi.

Einstein believed that if we don't know what time it is, we have no hope of figuring out where we are.

John and my dad, in the weeks leading up to the event, had poured footings and built the frame. What remained for our guests was to put the decking boards in place—to give us something to stand on. The photos are of John's dad running the chop saw, handing people boards cut just to the right length. Little nieces, dressed in pretty dresses, gathered around each other with hammers and nails and tried their best to drive them in straight. John's ninety-year-old grandmother, in one photo, with the sleeves of her delicate, white cardigan pushed up, wields a hammer. In other pictures (all taken by my father, the other wedding photographer in the family) my mother lays out food under a tent to feed the crew, and John's slew of adopted aunts fuss around the kitchen, keeping the coffee going.

With the last plank secured in place, I carried out baskets of hanging flowers I had ordered from the greenhouse down the road, hung them from the new railings, and the nieces scattered dried rose petals across the deck's blond surface. I changed into the ten-dollar wedding dress I had found in an online auction, and John put on a borrowed tuxedo. Because this was a non-wedding, we both wore Birkenstocks.

When we vowed to support, challenge, and teach one another, and then drove in the last nail of the deck together, I do believe, for that one moment, we meant it. All twenty fingers were wrapped around the shaft of that hammer, and we awkwardly drove that nail into the cedar. The pictures show us raising the hammer over our heads in triumph. We were promising only to try.

JUNE 2011

Kara and I met our justice of the peace under a sun so blinding that our sparse wedding photos show us in sunglasses. We had no witnesses, save a few vacationing families way down the beach and seagulls pacing the wet sand.

The justice of the peace we had found online arrived carrying the vows we had emailed to her. She squeezed our hands as we stood together on the sand, introducing ourselves. The open ocean was behind Kara and me until we turned to face each other. Then the offshore breezes came across our faces, lifting our hair. We both pushed our sunglasses onto our heads so we could see each other's eyes, and so I looked into the green eyes of my bride as she married me.

We vowed to support and challenge, teach and learn, sleep and arise together, in the spirit of bold adventure and love. Then she kissed me, just as I kissed her. And we were married.

We drove directly from the beach to an Indigo Girls concert on the western Maine border. By the time we slid into our seats with big glasses of wine in front of us, celebrating our marriage, we were unmarried.

We spent the night in a bed and breakfast down the road from the concert venue, and we slept a deep, exhausted sleep.

In the morning we rolled toward each other, our hands and lips immediately finding each other's skin. Around us the other guests were making their way down the inn's noisy, old wooden staircase to gather for breakfast. We moved silently together under the blankets, bringing each other to quiet climax, trying not to make noise, trying not to laugh. It didn't matter that here, on this soil, our union was illegal. We were married. I was making love to my wife now, not my girlfriend. And it felt different—more grounded. When I reached into her or put my lips to her neck, I did so knowing that she was the only person I would be this intimate with ever again, and that I was traveling sacred territory that was forever only mine. Sometimes, and this was one of those times, in her arms, as the orgasm starts to fade from my muscles, I cry openly. The relief of having landed in the safety of this piece of ground is too much to comprehend in these moments, and I cry.

JULY 2002

I lifted the stern end of the canoe, and John held the bow. We thumped it in place on top of my red Chevy Nova, strapped it down, taped a small "Just Married" sign in the back window, and drove across the bridge to Canada. We had no plan. The wedding, with its out-of-town guests and family we had not seen for a long time, had worn us both out, and we just wanted to drift.

We drove the numbingly uninteresting Trans-Canada Highway for a long time. John was at the wheel, and I rode with my feet on the dashboard, an atlas spread across my lap. Occasionally, another car honked, startling us into remembering the sign in the window.

Somewhere outside of St. John, we found a campground. It was on an island in the middle of a fat river. I drove the Nova on board a small ferry, and we rode from shore to the campground's entrance. Our site was at the edge of a pond, and before setting up our tent, we sat atop a picnic table watching beavers swim in and out of the domed structure they had built. The mound of branches and mud was impressive for its engineering—the strength and forethought that it took to build a home, a life.

We did not move for an hour, but when the sun had trekked its degrees across the sky long enough to motivate us, I walked to the small camp store to buy firewood, leaving John to set up the tent. It was the same gray tent I would later set aside when Kara and I bought the blue one from Sierra Designs. The floor of the camp store was smooth wood, worn down by years of campers' boots and sandals. I paid for a bundle of wood and a bag of ice, selected a box of sparklers and some matches. The clerk said, as she rang me up, "Are you the one with the 'Just Married' sign on your car?"

Once again, I had forgotten about it. "Yes," I answered, suddenly sheepish about it. Why had we chosen to advertise? What comfort were we drawing from it?

She smiled. "Congratulations!"

I smiled back. "Thank you." I still just felt so tired from the wedding, from the drive, from the loading and unloading of the canoe. It was going to take everything I had left just to carry this wood and ice back to our site. We needed fire and cold to get through the night.

Later that night, John and I paddled the canoe across the pond. I had packed dinner—cheese, bread, and a bottle of wine. We let the canoe drift while I poured wine and we toasted our life together. Someone was playing guitar and singing by their fire, and we listened. It was a folk song. Something we both knew. I sang along, softly. Above us, the New Brunswick sky had darkened, and constellations bloomed.

There is one circle in the night sky. Called the Winter Hexagon, this six-sided shape is made up of the brightest stars in other constellations, including Rigel, which lives in the knee of Orion, the hunter. It's referred to as the "Winter Hexagon, aka Winter Circle" throughout astronomy websites, and though that sounds like saying, "This is my cat, aka my dog," it's what the night sky offers.

There's also a square: the Great Square. It's made up of four stars of almost equal brightness, and though it's not square, it's closer to a square than a hexagon is to a circle, so in astronomy terms, its name is relatively accurate. The Great Square lives inside the constellation Pegasus.

The legends of Orion and Pegasus intersect. Pegasus, the great, winged horse, was the son of Poseidon and Medusa, the serpent-haired monster. Medusa was not always a monster, though. She was a beautiful young woman until Poseidon raped her in Athena's temple. An enraged Athena punished Medusa for being raped by making her so hideous that anyone who looked at her would turn to stone. The rape had left Medusa pregnant, and somehow her children sprang from her neck when the great hero Perseus decapitated her. As such, Pegasus is Poseidon's son.

Orion, a handsome hunter who could literally walk on water, was another son of Poseidon's. One time, Orion walked over to the island of Chios, where he got drunk and tried to force himself on Merope, the daughter of King Oenopion. The enraged king blinded Orion in retribution.

Zeus made the decisions about who became constellations and who didn't. Poor Medusa was not so rewarded, but her son Pegasus still sparkles and glints over our heads at night, and his brother, Orion, whose sight was restored after he walked east for a long time, was given a place and allowed to bring his two dogs with him. In other words, a man chose two other men (though, in fairness, one was a winged horse) to hover in the sky for eternity. One constellation, composing the Great Square, was the result of sexual violence. The other, who lends his knee to the Winter Circle, was a would-be perpetrator.

As John and I floated in our canoe and the guitar music faded into the darkness, the earth rotated, and these brothers, man and horse, traced diurnal circles above us, chasing each other in infinite loops around the celestial world as they had been ever since Zeus cast them there, allowing them to leave behind the violence that created them.

Deep notes from the bagpipes resonated in my chest. I was unprepared for that echoing, vibrating, and my heart rate sped up. My breathing too. My shoulders tensed, and I tightened my grip on the bundle of buttercups, paintbrush, and daisies. In front of me, an orchard of family members and friends had sprung up in the sloping field, and beyond them the Whiting Bay sparkled and rolled with the sun and tide. Kara stood somewhere behind me, over my shoulder, cheeks puffed out, blowing hard into her instrument. Abby and Owen waited in front of me, watching me for the signal to start our march. They each clutched handles of baskets filled with flower petals and were ready to sprinkle them in my path as I walked to the rock outcropping at the edge of the field. Our friend Judy stood there, sheaf of papers in her hand. The wailing of the pipes unfurled over our heads, passing through our bodies. I swallowed something that felt like a burst of sudden-onset crying, nodded to the kids, and we started walking the path to the altar.

This was our second wedding. We wore the same outfits, the same jewelry, and exchanged the same vows. This time, it included our people. Our parents. My kids. John. Our friends. Our siblings. And music. It included music. Of course.

Owen, six years old, sprinkled flower petals with concentration, the tip of his tongue sticking slightly out from between his lips while he worked. He wore a blue Hawaiian shirt, splashed with showy flowers. As we walked over the grasses and rocks, he placed each foot with the precision of a tightrope walker. Flower petals left his fingers with exquisite care, one at a time. Abby's approach was more carefree, much like the young woman she would later become. She barely watched where she put her feet. Eight years old, she made eye contact with people around her—charming the audience, letting the petals flutter from her fingertips.

The bagpipe music felt like matter, like a chute delivering me to the altar, like it was reducing me to particles that could pass intact through a wall. A woman who had known me since I was eleven years old reached out her arms in offer of a hug, and I paused in my march to accept. I leaned into her Patchouli-scented embrace, then straightened and kept walking.

To Judy's left, Kara's band's two other members waited for me. The fiddler's instrument was in rest position, held against his body with his arm. The other's guitar hung across his chest. My cello leaned against an empty chair. I reached them, handed Abby my flowers, sat, and took the cello between my knees. I lifted the bow, put it in position against the strings, and looked up at Kara. She reached the end of the measure and put the pipes down.

Our friends and family sat among blueberry plants, ferns, and young birch trees while John V., Jim, and I played. A beginning cello player still, I had practiced the tune all summer, even lugging the instrument to a week-long graduate school residency, playing it over and over each night before dropping off to sleep. My playing was tenuous, but the hairs of the bow gripped that first note exactly right, and Kara, now holding flowers, made her way down the same path through our people. She reached the rock, forever to be known as the wedding rock. I put the cello down and met her there.

We faced each other, held hands. The sun, not as blinding as it had been on the Cape, glinted off her dark hair. Judy rustled her papers. Charley read a Billy Collins poem. Rachel read a poem she composed from words our guests had sent in advance: three words per guest. Compassion. Trust. Faith. One, two, three, jump!

Afterward, there was potluck food, a chocolate wedding cake, and a keg of chestnut-brown Maine-brewed beer. People danced on the lawn. People set up tents in our front yard, so the celebration could continue in the morning, and nobody had to drive home. The band played late.

Our neighbor, on property adjacent to our own, let Kara and I use his cabin that night. It wasn't occupied; he lived downstate now and barely visited anymore. As the party's intensity began to slow, we excused ourselves and went to the cabin for the night. We wanted the privacy and the experience of waking up to that view of the sun rising above the bay, over the still morning water.

The walk to the cabin was close to a quarter mile of wooded trail, and we were tired and had been drinking. With headlamps on our foreheads, we navigated the trail, pushed open the cabin door, and quickly got into bed. We did not make love that night. We were too tired, too drunk, and entirely aware that we had the rest of our lives.

It could be said that, with this marriage, I not only came full circle, but I also squared the circle, an idiom that means to do the impossible. Achieving same sex marriage rights in Trump country could be seen as an example of squaring the circle. Likewise, so could exiting my identity only to find that my new identity was barely even a shade different. I had walked the Mobius strip and come back queer.

For ancient geometers, squaring the circle meant to create a square with the same area as a given circle, and they couldn't do it with the tools they had. The impossibility of the task is related to the role of pi when calculating the area of a circle. Pi is irrational and cannot conform to right angles and sides that match. Squares are solid. Grounded. Full of reason. To square is to be honest. To match up. Being square is to be predictable. Squares are a little self-righteous.

But that irrational, life-of-the-party, ever-expanding pi is in the DNA of the circle. Even modern mathematicians sound philosophical when they use the word "transcendental" to describe pi. That circles transcend all limits is made clear by humanity's reliance on them. The data is in, and people find circles more pleasing than all the other shapes, but you don't need scientific findings to see it. The circle of life, mandalas, Stonehenge, yin and yang, the tree of life, the Ouroboros (the snake that eats its own tail), the Dharma wheel, wedding rings, Olympic rings.

It's not lost on me that, despite our infatuation with soft edges, squares are the foundation of our domestic lives. In Michael Pollen's book *A Place of My Own*, in which he builds a small cabin, some small part of the building's frame is fastened together without being squared off. That minor-seeming error chases him through the rest of the project, as every other piece of the building—all the way through to the interior finish work—is made to compensate for that one cockeyed joint to achieve squareness, squareness being essential for structural integrity. Though humans are irrational, transcendent circles, our bank balances have to square with our credits and debits. Our commitments are slotted into the grid-like structure of our days. Insurance forms, report cards, self-addressed stamped envelopes, shopping lists, and child custody agreements are right-angled and sharp. If any one of those things slips out of square, the difference will chase us our whole lives. The years move by in cycles, but calendars are grids.

It was 1913 when Wassily Kandinsky first stacked circles atop one another and lined them up in boxes of squares. Ten years later he painted *Circles in a Circle*, a piece in which the circles are running amok and the squares have been demolished, leaving a detritus of scattered straight lines. His need for transcendence and irrationality expanded and outgrew the confines of the grid, and the circles became free.

# Impossible Objects

I printed out the PDF template that I found online. It promised to make construction of the famed Impossible triangle, also called the Penrose triangle, achievable in less than five minutes, ten at the most. I printed nine copies of the PDF on red card stock because it seemed that—for a triangle—I would need three, and I wanted room for error. I also imagined that it would be so fun and easy that my kids would want to construct their own. I sat, on a Sunday, with scissors and tape and nine pieces of card stock, ready to create something impossible.

Impossible objects are considered by some to be synonymous with optical illusions, but the effect comes from somewhere well beyond the workings of our eyeballs. It's the brain, informed by lived experience and expectations formed therein, that fills in the gaps. Take Escher's famous staircase, in which one flight of stairs climbs to meet another, which hooks a right and climbs to meet a third, and then the fourth staircase hooks back to the first one, and they are all ascending: our experience brains make peace with the lack of a descent over the objection of our logic brains. The three-dimensional legs of the Impossible triangle fold between and through each other in a way unbecoming of reality. It can't be done except through the trick of two-dimensional drawing. Our minds do the rest.

The shape was first created by a Swedish artist but was made famous by a psychiatrist, Lionel Penrose, and his mathematician son, Roger. Penrose the younger described the Penrose triangle as "impossibility in its purest form." To me, it sounds like the beginning of a bad joke: an artist, a psychiatrist, and a mathematician walk into a bar, but the punchline is an iconic image of a three-sided, two-dimensional object that's as impossible as every part of my life so far.

With crappy, blue-handled scissors I found jammed into the jar of pens that didn't write that we kept next to the phone, I excavated the shape—three times—from the card stock. I folded along the dotted lines and regarded the shapes there where they balanced on their edges, looking a little like a trio of damaged, red giraffes. I held one up against another, turned it, tried again, leaned the two of them against the third. Separated them, reunited them, rotated them, scooted them around.

Our dog spread his bulk underneath the dining room table and slowly let out a groan as I entered my second hour. I took breaks. I ate an apple and stared out the window. I checked Facebook over and over. I grew angry at the website from which I had downloaded the PDF for its shitty instructions and empty promises of ease.

I determined, early, that I didn't need three cutouts. Somehow, this was supposed to happen with just one.

I swept the dining room and unloaded the dishwasher. I poured a glass of iced coffee, and I sat and regarded this paper object where it mocked me from the tabletop. It would never be a three-dimensional triangle. Beyond the edges of the table, the open floor plan of our house provided a cacophony of possible objects. Rice cooker. Rocking chair. Recycling bin. Shoe rack. Laundry basket. They are possible because they occupy all three dimensions. The thing I was trying to make occupied only two but had aspirations. The trick had to be in the eye of the looker. I had to let it fool me.

I flipped it over in my hands, made it face me backward. There's a trick of light that can make objects flip around backward without touching them, and I wonder if that would have helped. Slide a clear glass of water in front of an arrow pointing to the left, and the light refracts, tricking our eyes into seeing that the arrow now points to the right. This classic optical illusion was once used in an anti–drunk driving ad: a road sign with a bent arrow indicating that the road turns right is placed behind a drinking glass, and as the glass is filled with alcohol the arrow lies to the drinker by flipping itself around. Any person trying to see through the alcohol is unable to see the truth about the road ahead. Ultimately, that was the case for me. Over many years—years that extend far beyond the scope of this story—increasing alcohol use refracted my world and all the objects in it until I didn't know which direction any of the arrows pointed, and I couldn't tell what way I was supposed to go. By the time I was trimming away card stock to release the Impossible triangle from its two-dimensional existence, I had spent years tucked into a comfortable chair in the office of a smart therapist who had asked hard questions she already knew the answers to and helped me see that the arrows pointed the way across the bridge to sobriety. After all that time, I knew how to adjust my view to get a better look at reality.

I placed the shape on one folded edge, balanced it, walked away, turned back to look at it. I squinted. I tossed it on the floor, not caring how it landed. I tilted my head. It insisted on looking like a mangled—and very possible—piece of cut-up red card stock.

I furiously Googled, searching for more specific directions, and I found some in Perth, Australia. In a grassy roundabout at the intersection of Bennett and Plain, cars took tight turns around a forty-four-foot-high sculpture of the Penrose triangle. Viewed from most angles, it looked like a shining, metal version of the gangly, red card stock creation on my table, but a series of photographs showed how to walk around it and where to stand so that the illusion would pop into being. One blogger described that standing spot as a "death trap for pedestrians," but someone must have stood there because there—on the internet—was the answer. The answer was not in manipulating the object. The answer was to change perspective.

I took a step back. With my right eye closed, I squinted my left eye until my vision blurred. With only one eye, vision becomes two-dimensional. I climbed onto a chair and leaned a little left then a little right. I climbed off the chair and moved it farther away from the object, then climbed back on. I leaned and half-turned away, trying to see it using only the corner of my eye. With my body held in this untenable position, the Penrose triangle popped into an out-of-focus state of possibility. It hovered like a hologram, one leg vanishing behind another, like a knot. I stiffened myself into the sweet spot where the vision shimmered intact—my body leaning forward, maintaining balance on the seat of the chair. To see it, I had to back up. I had to shift.

## ACKNOWLEDGMENTS

Nobody should write alone.

Thank you to the Sarahs (Sarah Einstein and Sarah Twombly), who each read versions of this manuscript and relayed their feedback to versions of me. Thank you to Alexis Paige for being my sister in writerly neuroses. Thank you to Barbara Hurd, Debra Marquart, Aaron Hamburger, and Suzanne Strempek Shea, my mentors at Stonecoast MFA, who responded, redirected, refined, and reassured this work and its hapless author. (You were all disturbingly, annoyingly right. Every time.) Thank you to Judy Pratt for luring me over from the fiction side. Thank you to Kevin Sample for helping me find my way back to myself when I was lost. (You were also disturbingly, annoyingly right. Every time.) Thank you to all the editors of all the literary magazines who gave my work some real estate and an audience. Thank you to Abigail Thomas for her generosity of spirit. Thank you to Courtney Ochsner at the University of Nebraska Press for saying yes. Thank you to my agent, Michele Mortimer, for tirelessly helping me make this book better and for giving me the ability to use the phrase "my agent." Lastly, thank you to Sarah, Annie, Emily, and Laurie—my far-flung writing group—for buoying me across the times and through the things.

Thank you. Thank you. Thank you.

## In the American Lives Series

*Between Panic and Desire*
by Dinty W. Moore

*To Hell with It: Of Sin and Sex,*
*Chicken Wings, and Dante's*
*Entirely Ridiculous, Needlessly*
*Guilt-Inducing "Inferno"*
by Dinty W. Moore

*Let Me Count the Ways:*
*A Memoir*
by Tomás Q. Morín

*Shadow Migration:*
*Mapping a Life*
by Suzanne Ohlmann

*Meander Belt: Family, Loss,*
*and Coming of Age in the*
*Working-Class South*
by M. Randal O'Wain

*Sleep in Me*
by Jon Pineda

*The Solace of Stones: Finding*
*a Way through Wilderness*
by Julie Riddle

*Works Cited: An Alphabetical*
*Odyssey of Mayhem and*
*Misbehavior*
by Brandon R. Schrand

*Thoughts from a*
*Queen-Sized Bed*
by Mimi Schwartz

*My Ruby Slippers:*
*The Road Back to Kansas*
by Tracy Seeley

*The Fortune Teller's Kiss*
by Brenda Serotte

*Gang of One: Memoirs of*
*a Red Guard*
by Fan Shen

*Just Breathe Normally*
by Peggy Shumaker

*How to Survive Death and*
*Other Inconveniences*
by Sue William Silverman

*The Pat Boone Fan Club:*
*My Life as a White*
*Anglo-Saxon Jew*
by Sue William Silverman

*Scraping By in the Big Eighties*
by Natalia Rachel Singer

*Sky Songs: Meditations on*
*Loving a Broken World*
by Jennifer Sinor

*In the Shadow of Memory*
by Floyd Skloot

*Secret Frequencies:*
*A New York Education*
by John Skoyles

*The Days Are Gods*
by Liz Stephens

*Phantom Limb*
by Janet Sternburg

*This Jade World*
by Ira Sukrungruang

*The Sound of Undoing:*
*A Memoir in Essays*
by Paige Towers

*When We Were Ghouls:*
*A Memoir of Ghost Stories*
by Amy E. Wallen

*Knocked Down:*
*A High-Risk Memoir*
by Aileen Weintraub

*Yellowstone Autumn: A Season of*
*Discovery in a Wondrous Land*
by W. D. Wetherell

*This Fish Is Fowl:*
*Essays of Being*
by Xu Xi

To order or obtain more information on these or other
University of Nebraska Press titles, visit nebraskapress.unl.edu.